符号中国 SIGNS OF CHINA

中国名山

FAMOUS MOUNTAINS IN CHINA

"符号中国"编写组 ◎ 编著

中央民族大学出版社
China Minzu University Press

图书在版编目(CIP)数据

中国名山：汉文、英文／"符号中国"编写组编著． —北京：中央民族大学出版社，2024.3
（符号中国）
ISBN 978-7-5660-2284-4

Ⅰ.①中… Ⅱ.①符… Ⅲ.①山—介绍—中国—汉、英 Ⅳ.①K928.3

中国国家版本馆CIP数据核字（2024）第016760号

符号中国：中国名山 FAMOUS MOUNTAINS IN CHINA

编　　著	"符号中国"编写组
策划编辑	沙　平
责任编辑	李苏幸
英文指导	李瑞清
英文编辑	邱　械
美术编辑	曹　娜　郑亚超　洪　涛
出版发行	中央民族大学出版社
	北京市海淀区中关村南大街27号　邮编：100081
	电话：（010）68472815（发行部）　传真：（010）68933757（发行部）
	（010）68932218（总编室）　　　　（010）68932447（办公室）
经销者	全国各地新华书店
印刷厂	北京兴星伟业印刷有限公司
开　　本	787 mm×1092 mm　1/16　印张：10.625
字　　数	139千字
版　　次	2024年3月第1版　2024年3月第1次印刷
书　　号	ISBN 978-7-5660-2284-4
定　　价	58.00元

版权所有　侵权必究

"符号中国"丛书编委会

唐兰东　巴哈提　杨国华　孟靖朝　赵秀琴

本册编写者

王　佳

前 言 Preface

　　中国历史悠久，幅员辽阔，其中三分之二的国土是山地、高原和丘陵，自古便是一个多山之国。这些山遍布大江南北，或灵秀仙逸，或巍峨雄壮，或陡峭险峻，呈现出变化多端的自然景观，装点了巍巍中华的锦绣大地。

　　自古以来，中国人就对名山怀有崇拜和敬畏之情。从四千年前的夏朝就

China is a country with a long history and a vast territory. Two thirds of its land is characterized by mountains, plateaux and hills. Since ancient times, China has always been a mountainous country. Mountain ranges spread across both the north and south of the country, some elegant, some magnificent, and some precipitous. The beautiful land of China is embellished with the ever-changing natural scenery of these mountains.

　　The Chinese have always adored and been awed by mountains since time immemorial. There are many legends about famous mountains in China going as far back as four thousand years ago in the Xia Dynasty (2070 B.C.-1600 B.C.). After the Spring and Autumn Period (770 B.C.-476

1

有许多关于名山的传说。春秋之后的历代皇帝更是将祭祀山岳、巡山封禅作为新帝登基、祈佑盛世的重要活动。他们认为山就是自然的代表，也是一切神灵休养生息的地方。因此，名山是中国古代神话和传说最为丰富的地方。也正因为如此，名山成了中国佛教、道教、儒教的修心求法之地。山上建造的殿宇楼亭、寺庙塔窟，以及怪洞奇潭、蔽日古木，还有代代传承的精神文化，这些都是名山的宝贵财富。

尽管时光荏苒，朝代更替，名山依然以巍峨壮观的身躯纵横在中华的大地之上，记录着中华民族上下五千年的历史文化，是人类财富中不可磨灭的丰碑。

现在，就让我们一同领略中国名山的雄伟风姿，感受它们深厚的文化底蕴。

B.C.), rituals to worship mountains and offer sacrifices to heaven during mountain visits became important activities of each dynasty when a new emperor ascended the throne to celebrate upcoming prosperity and peace. Mountains were also considered a symbol of nature and the dwelling and self-cultivation places for divinities and immortals. Therefore, mountains were the source of the richest and the most legendary Chinese ancient myths and folklores. Precisely for the same reason, mountains became places where Buddhists, Taoists or Confucianists practiced self-cultivation to seek the truth. Temples, pagodas, pavilions, peculiarly shaped caverns and ponds, ancient forests and the spiritual culture passed down through generations are all valuable assets of these famous mountains.

With time passing, dynasties replaced one another. These magnificent mountains across the vast lands of China recorded five thousand years of Chinese history and culture, and became a permanent monument of mankind's wealth.

Let us walk through the splendid and grandeur scenic sites of these famous mountains and enjoy their manifestation of the deep Chinese cultural heritage.

目录 Contents

三山五岳
Three Great Mountains and Five Sacred Mountains 001

中国第一奇山——黄山
No. 1 Unique Mountain in China:
Mount Huang (*Huang Shan*) 002

奇秀甲天下——庐山
Peculiar Beauty in the World:
Mount Lu (*Lu Shan*) 015

东南第一山——雁荡山
No. 1 Mountain in Southeast China:
Mount Yandang (*Yandang Shan*) 026

东岳泰山
East Sacred Mountain:
Mount Tai (*Tai Shan*) 036

中岳嵩山
Central Sacred Mountain:
Mount Song (*Song Shan*) 050

南岳衡山
South Sacred Mountain: Mount Heng
(*Heng Shan*, Hunan Province) 060

西岳华山
West Sacred Mountain: Mount Hua
(*Hua Shan*) 067

北岳恒山
North Sacred Mountain: Mount Heng
(*Heng Shan*, Shanxi) 077

佛教名山
Famous Buddhist Mountains 089

五台山
Mount Wutai (*Wutai Shan*) 090

峨眉山
Mount Emei (*Emei Shan*) 100

九华山
Mount Jiuhua (*Jiuhua Shan*) 111

普陀山
Mount Putuo (*Putuo Shan*) 120

道教名山
Famous Taoist Mountains 127

武当山
Mount Wudang (*Wudang Shan*) 128

青城山
Mount Qingcheng (*Qingcheng Shan*) 136

齐云山
Mount Qiyun (*Qiyun Shan*) 144

龙虎山
Mount Longhu (*Longhu Shan*) 155

三山五岳
Three Great Mountains and Five Sacred Mountains

　　"三山五岳"是中国8座著名的大山,不仅风景壮观,且具有深厚的文化底蕴。三山指黄山、庐山和雁荡山;五岳指泰山、华山、衡山、嵩山和恒山。

Three Great Mountains and Five Sacred Mountains (*Sanshan Wuyue*) refer to the eight most famous mountains of magnificent scenery and rich culture heritage in China. The three mountains are Mount Huang (*Huang Shan*), Mount Lu (*Lu Shan*) and Mount Yandang (*Yandang Shan*). The five sacred mountains are Mount Tai (*Tai Shan*), Mount Hua (*Hua Shan*), Mount Heng (*Heng Shan*, Hunan Province), Mount Song (*Song Shan*) and Mount Heng (*Heng Shan*, Shanxi Province).

> 中国第一奇山——黄山

黄山雄踞于安徽省南部，南北约40公里，东西约30公里，风景区方圆154平方公里，总面积约1200平方公里，历史上号称"五百里黄山"，是中国三山五岳之中的三山之一，并与长江、长城、黄河并称为中华民族的象征。

黄山由于山色黝黑，古称"黟山"。相传中华民族的祖先轩辕黄帝被黟山秀美的风光所吸引，于是率领手下大臣容成子和浮丘公来此，以石为臼，并吸取山中仙气，以炼仙丹。唐天宝六年(747年)，唐明皇根据这个传说，将黟山改名为"黄山"。至今，黄山依然留有这三位仙人的众多遗迹，其中

> No. 1 Unique Mountain in China: Mount Huang (*Huang Shan*)

Mount Huang (*Huang Shan*, literally Yellow Mountain) locates in the south of Anhui province, and it covers a total of 1200 square kilometers stretching 40 kilometers from north to south and 30 kilometers from east to west with a well-developed scenic area of 154 square kilometers. Historically it was acclaimed as "Five Hundred *Li* of *Huang Shan*" (*Li*, the unit of length in China, is equal to 0.5 km). Mount Huang is one of the three great mountains in China and considered a symbol of the Chinese nationality together with the Great Wall, the Yangtze River and the Yellow River.

Mount Huang was originally known as *Yi Shan* (meaning Black Mountain) owing to its dark landscape. It is said

七十二峰中耸立云端的轩辕峰、浮丘峰和容成峰，就是以他们的名字命名的。

黄山素有"中国第一奇山"之誉，山脉自东北向西南绵延250公里，山势险峻，境内呈峰林状，千峰万岭，峥嵘嶙峋，其中有名可数的就有三十六大峰、三十六小峰。这些山峰以天都峰、莲花峰、光明顶三大主峰为中心向四周铺展，错落有致，高低起伏。峰峦峭壁崔

that the Chinese ancestor Emperor Huang was fascinated by *Huang Shan*'s beautiful scenery, so he brought his ministers Rongchengzi and Fuqiugong to make elixir in a stone mortar filled with celestial energy. In the year 747, Emperor Xuanzong of the Tang Dynasty changed the name *Yi Shan* to *Huang Shan* based on this legend. Today there are still many historical sites in Mount Huang about these three immortals. Among the seventy-two towering peaks in Mount Huang, Peak Xuanyuan, Peak Rongcheng and Peak Fuqiu were named after them.

Known as the "No. 1 Unique Mountain" in China, Mount Huang's mountain range stretches 250 kilometers from northeast to southwest featuring landforms of numerous sheer cliffs, imposing peaks and grotesquely shaped rocks. The most well-known peaks include thirty-six big peaks and thirty-six small peaks. The three highest peaks are Heavenly Capital Peak (*Tiandu Feng*), Lotus Blossom Peak (*Lianhua Feng*) and Brightness Summit (*Guangming Ding*), around which other

- 黄山风光
Scenery of Mount Huang

• 群峰林立的黄山
Towering Peaks in Mount Huang

崇雄浑，深壑幽谷天然巧成。山中林木茂密，古树繁多，森林覆盖率达86.6%，有植物近1500种，动物500多种。置身山中，一时一景都奇妙瑰丽，引人入胜，尤其以"奇松、怪石、云海、温泉"四绝闻名天下。黄山的奇伟丽景吸引了古今

smaller ones spread out and undulate throughout the mountain range layer by layer, presenting a natural spectacle of steep and cliffy mountain peaks with deep and quiet valleys. Predominantly evergreen forests characterized by ancient pine trees cover 86.6% of the entire mountain, which has close to 1,500 plants and over 500 animal species. Once in the mountain range, it is easy to immerse oneself in this magical scenery, particularly by the four best scenic spots: extraordinary pine trees, grotesque rocks, sea of clouds, and bubbling hot springs. The beautiful scenery of Mount Huang has attracted numerous notable figures of all times from China and abroad. Xu Xiake exclaimed in his *Travel Diaries of Xu Xiake* that "nothing in the world can be compared with *Huang Shan* in Anhui; once in *Huang Shan*, no mountain is worth climbing." Later another saying even claimed that "if one visited the five sacred mountains, there is no need to see another mountain; if one visited Huang Shan, there is no need to visit the

中外无数名人雅士登临。徐霞客曾在《徐霞客游记》里感叹道："薄海内外无如徽之黄山,登黄山天下无山,观止矣。"后来更有人称"五岳归来不看山,黄山归来不看岳",给黄山以极高的评价。

黄山不仅以巍峨壮丽、奇幻多姿著称于世,还是中国古代的道教和佛教圣地。山中人文景观历史悠久,文化深厚。现存各种亭阁、寺庙、摩崖石刻多达280余处,朱砂峰、炼丹峰、望仙台等均以道教传统命名,自然风光与人文景观和谐共荣。

five sacred mountains", giving very high praise of it.

Mount Huang is not only well-known for its majestic and mysterious scenic beauty, but also as a sacred site of Buddhist and Taoist in ancient China. Its landscape features over 280 pavilions, pagodas, temples and rock inscriptions with deep-rooted culture and a long history. Cinnabar Peak (*Zhusha Feng*), Alchemy Peak (*Liandan Feng*) and Watching Fairy Terrace (*Wangxian Tai*) are named after Taoism traditions, which demonstrate harmony between the natural and cultural landscape.

• 雪后黄山远眺
Overlooking Mount Huang after Snow

徐霞客与《徐霞客游记》

徐霞客是明代伟大的地理学家、旅行家和探险家。从1608年开始，徐霞客先后游历了今天的江苏、安徽、浙江、山东等18个省，足迹遍及大半个中国，历时34年。在游历的过程中，他每天都会将自己考察的收获记录下来，共240多万字，可惜大多散佚了。留下来的游记经后人整理成书，名为《徐霞客游记》，这是中国最早的一部比较详细地记录所经地理环境的游记，也是世界上最早记述岩溶地貌并详细考证其成因的书籍。《徐霞客游记》共40多万字，对地理、水文、地质、植物等方面的内容，均有详细阐述，在地理学和文学上都卓有成就。

Xu Xiake and *Travel Diaries of Xu Xiake*

Xu Xiake was a great geographer, traveller, explorer, and in the Ming Dynasty (1368-1644). Starting from 1608 he traveled to 18 provinces and regions including Jiangsu, Anhui, Zhejiang and Shangdong in 34 years almost halfway across China. On his journey throughout China he documented his visits everyday in a total of over 2.4 million Chinese characters. Unfortunately most of his notes were lost and those left behind were compiled later into a book titled *Travel Diaries of Xu Xiake*. This book became the earliest travel notes in China documenting extensively about geographical environments and the earliest research work in the world that documented Karst landform and examined its causes in details. In over 400,000 Chinese characters it describes in great details about the geography, hydrology, geology and vegetation. It is considered an accomplished book in both geography and literature.

- **黄山始信峰**

始信峰凸起于绝壑之上，海拔1683米。此峰三面临空，小巧玲珑，风姿独秀。

Beginning to Believe Peak (*Shixin Feng*) of Mount Huang

This small and elegant peak stands out from the clefts of the mountain with sheer cliffs on three sides at an altitude of 1,683 meters.

奇松

古人曰："黄山之美始于松。"黄山松是由于黄山的独特地貌、气候而形成的中国松树的一个变种。黄山松的针叶短粗稠密，叶色浓绿，枝干曲生，树冠扁平，显出一种朴实、稳健、雄浑的气势。而每一处、每一株松树，在形态、

- 黄山松

黄山松生长在黄山的岩石间，扎根于巨岩裂隙，以无坚不摧、有缝即入的钻劲，在山上发芽、生根、成长。

Pine Trees in Mount Huang
The Mount Huang pine sprouts, roots and grows in the rock crevices, tough and persistent.

Extraordinary Pine Trees

An ancient saying goes, "the beauty of Mount Huang starts from its pine trees." Pine trees in Mount Huang are variants of the Chinese pine tree family as a result of the unique geomorphology and climate in Mount Huang. They are evergreen trees with very broad, flat-topped crowns of long, twisted branches and needle-like, thick and short leaves. They present an earthy, strong and forceful impression. Each pine tree depending on where it grows has a different shape and charm, showing an unusual beauty. Elegant

冬季的黄山松
Mount Huang Pine in Winter

气韵上又各有不同，都有一种奇特的美。人们根据它们不同的形态和神韵，为它们分别起了贴切自然而又典雅有趣的名字，如迎客松、黑虎松、探海松、团结松等等。黄山松以坚硬的花岗岩石为壤，或迎风挺立于峰顶，或悬于悬崖峭壁，或隐于深壑幽谷，郁郁葱葱，焕发出无限的生机，与黄山奇特的自然景观相映成趣，形成了"无峰不石，无石不松，无松不奇"的秀丽景色。

and interesting names were given to them based on their different shapes and charms such as Greeting Pine (*Yingke Song*), Black Tiger Pine (*Heihu Song*), Exploring Sea Pine (*Tanhai Song*), and Unity Pine (*Tuanjie Song*). These pine trees grow straight out of hard rocks; some stand on the mountain peak braving the wind; some reach out from cliff; and some hide in the deep valley. Their lush green glows in vitality existing side by side with Mount Huang's natural landscape forming a scenic beauty of "no peak without rocks, no rocks without a pine, and no pine is an ordinary pine."

怪石

　　黄山石的特点是象形，有的像人，有的又形似动植物，造型别致，活灵活现，给人以丰富的想象空间，再佐以情趣盎然的青山绿水，更加意趣无穷。这些奇山怪石形态逼真，或与奇松相依相偎，或与云雾缠绵共舞，构成了一幅幅天然的画卷，令人深入山中流连忘返。黄山的怪石数不胜数，有猴子观海、仙人下棋、仙人指路、梦笔生花、笔架峰、飞来石等，这些意趣盎然的石头又因种种美丽的神话传说为黄山增添了许多意境之美。

Grotesque Rocks

Rocks in Mount Huang are figurative. Some look like human beings and some like animals. The shape of rock are vivid and unique giving visitors plenty of room for imagination. They become more interesting when embraced by green mountains and clear water. Possessing a realistic style, some of these grotesque rocks stand side by side with ancient gnarled pine trees, some are surrounded by misty clouds. They created a series of natural Chinese scroll paintings, making the visitors enjoy themselves in Mount Huang so much as to forget to leave. There are numerous grotesque rocks in Mount Huang, such as the famous "A Monkey Looking at the Sea" (*Houzi Guanhai*), Immortals Playing Chest (*Xianren Xiaqi*), Immortals Pointing the Way (*Xianren Zhilu*), Flowers Growing Out of a Writing Brush (*Mengbi Shenghua*), Pen Rack Peak (*Bijia Feng*) and Rock that Flew from Afar (*Feilai Shi*). The legends and mysteries about these interesting rocks give additional beauty of artistic conception to Mount Huang.

● 黄山飞来石
飞来石位于黄山光明顶的西北方，呈近长方柱体耸立在峰头基岩平台之上，高15米。

Rock that Flew From Afar in Mount Huang
This rock is located at northwest of the Brightness Summit. It is 15 meters high in a rectangular shape standing out on a flat area on top of the peak.

云海

　　云海是黄山第一奇观，故黄山又被称为"云海之都"。黄山多云雾，一年之中有200多天都是湿度极大的天气。这些水汽蒸发升腾遇冷，就会形成云山雾海。站在山顶登高俯瞰，只见身外云海波澜壮阔，一望无边。那些流云随着风隐隐翻腾流动，忽而如巨浪击山，忽而风平浪静，变化多端，捉摸不透。而黄山的大小山峰、千沟万壑都淹没在这苍茫的云海之中，如同大海中漂泊不定的渔船，被那些或

Sea of Clouds

The sea of clouds is acclaimed the No. 1 wonder of Mount Huang, thus making Mount Huang known as "the city of seas of clouds". The weather of Mount Huang is cloudy and foggy, with high humidity over 200 days in a year. When moisture rises then hit the cold air, it forms a sea of misty clouds. When looking downward from the top of the mountain, one sees an ever-changing and unpredictable view of endless waves of clouds churning and rolling; in one moment a big wave of clouds hit the mountain peaks; in another moment everything quiets down.

• 黄山云海
黄山一年之中大雾弥漫的天气有200多天，水汽升腾或雨后雾气未消，波翻浪涌，这就更增添了云海的壮阔。

Sea of Clouds in Mount Huang
Mount Huang has over 200 days of heavy fog in a year. The sea of clouds becomes more magnificent when water evaporates and mist still lingers after the rain.

● 黄山温泉 (图片提供：FOTOE)
Hot Spring in Mount Huang

绵绵或厚实的云浪拍击成绿的碎片。即使一些海拔较高的山峰，如天都峰、光明顶等山峰，也都淹没在这浩瀚无边的雾气中，成为云中孤岛。中国现代文人郭沫若称赞其"瞬息万变万万变，忽隐忽现，或浓或淡，胜似梦境之迷离"。

温泉

黄山温泉出自海拔850米紫云峰，历史悠久，名扬天下。据宋代的《黄山图经》记载，传说中华民族的始祖轩辕黄帝曾在此沐浴七七四十九天，这里的温泉

Thousands of peaks, ridges and valleys, big and small, are all submerged in this vast sea of clouds as if they are fishing boats wandering in the sea and broken into green pieces by continuously coming thick waves. Even some of the highest peaks such as the Celestial Capital Peak and the Brightness Summit become isolated islands in this vast expanse of misty clouds. The well-known Chinese scholar and writer Guo Moruo commended this phenomenon, "the ever-changing the sea of clouds is like a misted dream having thousands of transformations with dense or light scenery all flickering in one moment."

因此名声大振。黄山温泉共有15处，位于紫石峰南麓，汤泉溪北岸，海拔650米处，自唐朝起就已经开发。由于温泉流量稳定，常年保持42℃左右。相传温泉源头来自朱砂峰，峰下有洞，洞中产朱砂，因此称为"朱砂泉"。

Bubbling Hot Springs

Bubbling hot spring sites are located below the Purple Cloud Peak (*Ziyun Feng*) at an altitude of 850 meters. These hot springs have long history, and they are well known in China. According to the *Geological Records of Mount Huang* in the Song Dynasty, the Chinese ancestor Emperor Huang bathed in a hot spring for forty-nine days. thus making hot springs in Mount Huang very famous. There are 15 hot spring sites located between the southern foot of the Purple Cloud Peak (*Ziyun Feng*) and the northern bank of the Spring Creek (*Tangquan Xi*) at 650 meters above sea level and they have been developed since the Tang Dynasty. Thanks to the constant and stable flow of hot spring water, the temperature remains at around 42°C all year round. It is said that the source of the hot springs comes from Cinnabar Peak. There is a cave under the peak and cinnabar is produced in the cave, hence the name "Cinnabar Spring" in ancient times.

- 《黄山胜景》（清 石涛）
Scenic Beauty of Mount Huang by Shi Tao, Qing Dynasty (1616-1911)

送温处士归黄山白鹅峰旧居（唐 李白）

黄山四千仞，三十二莲峰。
丹崖夹石柱，菡萏金芙蓉。
伊昔升绝顶，下窥天目松。
仙人炼玉处，羽化留余踪。
亦闻温伯雪，独往今相逢。
采秀辞五岳，攀岩历万重。
归休白鹅岭，渴饮丹砂井。
凤吹我时来，云车尔当整。
去去陵阳东，行行芳桂丛。
回溪十六度，碧嶂尽晴空。
他日还相访，乘桥蹑彩虹。

诗词译文：

黄山高耸足有四千仞，各峰如莲花般簇拥着三十二峰。
绮丽的岩壁形态各异，有的像莲花苞，有的像金芙蓉。
忆往昔，我曾登临绝顶，放眼远眺天目山上的老松。
仙人炼玉的遗迹尚在，羽化升仙处还留有遗踪。
我知道今天你要独自去往黄山，或许可以与温伯雪（李白的好友）相逢。
为了采撷精华辞别五岳，攀岩临穴，经历艰险千万重。
归来闲居白鹅岭上，渴了饮丹砂井中的水。
凤凰叫时我即来，你要准备云霓车驾，与我一同游览天宫。
来往陵阳仙山东，行走在芬芳的桂树丛中。
回曲溪流十六渡，青山如嶂立晴空。
以后我还会时常来拜访，乘着弓桥步入彩虹中。

Sending Wen Chushi Off to His Old Residence on White Goose Peak in Huang Shan by Li Bai, Tang Dynasty (618-907)

Poem Interpretation

Huang Shan is as high as 4000 feet surrounded by 32 peaks like lotus blossoms;

Enchanting ridges and cliffs have a great variety of shapes: some look like lotus buds and some golden hibiscus;

Recalling the past I once ascended to the top of the mountain overlooking ancient pine trees in Mount Tianmu;

The relics showing how immortals refined jade and places they ascended heaven still exist;

I know you will be off to Huang Shan alone today, perhaps meeting Wen Boxue on your way;

Having gone through hardships and dangers you climb up high and enjoy the best view, and say farewell to five sacred mountains;

Return to White Goose Peak for a leisure living and when thirsty drink cinnabar spring water from the well;

I will come when the phoenix calls, have the cloud carriage prepared and we will tour the palace of heaven together;

Come to the eastern of Lingyang mountain range to stroll in the midst of sweet osmanthus fragrance;

Around the creeks with sixteen turns, when the sky is clear all green mountains are captured in the eyes;

I will come and visit you crossing the arch bridge into the rainbow.

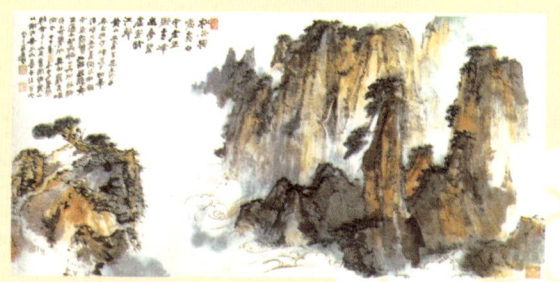

- 《黄山文笔峰图轴》（现代 张大千）
  Scroll Painting of Writing Brush Peak(Wengbi Feng) of Mount Huang, Zhang Daqiang, Modern

> 奇秀甲天下——庐山

　　庐山位于江西省九江市以南，耸立于鄱阳湖、长江之滨。其风光以"奇、秀、险、雄"闻名于世，唐代大诗人白居易曾予以"匡庐奇秀甲天下"的美誉，赞扬庐山秀美为名山之首。

　　庐山又叫"匡庐""匡山"。相传周朝时有一位叫匡俗的先生在庐山研究道学的仙术，被周天子获知。周天子屡次遣人请他出山相助，但匡俗每次都潜入深山之中，避而不见，数次之后，再不可觅。人们纷纷传说他已成仙而去。于是便把匡俗求仙的地方称为"神仙之庐"，"庐山"这一名称由此而来。

　　庐山是一座地垒式断块山，东西两侧为大断裂，山体多峭壁悬崖，具有河流、湖泊、坡地、山峰

> Peculiar Beauty in the World: Mount Lu (*Lu Shan*)

Mount Lu is situated in south of Jiujiang City in Jiangxi Province. It neighbors Poyang Lake to the east, and the Yangtze River to the north. The scenery of Mount Lu is well-known for its peculiarity, elegance, precipitousness and magnificence. Bai Juyi, one of the greatest poets of the Tang Dynasty lauded it as the best of China's famous mountains: "The peculiar beauty of *Kuanglu* is peerless in the world."

　　Mount Lu was also called *Kuanglu* or *Kuang Shan*. It is said that a scholar named Kuangsu who studied divination practices of Taoism in Mount Lu, the King of Zhou Dynasty sent people to invite him to assist the King many times. But Kuangsu hiding in the deep mountain refused to come out and meet

等多种地貌，相对高度1200—1400米。主峰汉阳峰，海拔1474米。庐山现今302平方公里的风景区内，自古命名的山峰便有171座。群峰间散布冈岭26座，壑谷20条，岩洞16个，怪石22处。水流在河谷处发育裂点，形成许多急流与瀑布，瀑布22处，溪涧18条，湖潭14处。著名的三叠泉瀑布，落差达155米。庐山主要风景名胜有五老峰、三叠泉、含鄱口、芦林湖、大天池、花径、如琴湖、锦绣谷、仙人洞、小天

the King. Since he was nowhere to be found, rumors spread that he ascended heaven and became an immortal. Thus the place where he practiced divinations for immortality was called the "Celestial *Lu*" (meaning celestial cottage), hence the name *Lu Shan*.

The mountain range of Mount Lu has horst and graben topography with two big faults in the east and the west. It has a stunning landscape of sheer cliffs and peaks, and various landforms like rivers, lakes and sloping fields at an altitude between 1,200 and 1,400 meters. The

• 庐山风光
Scenery of Mount Lu

● 庐山风光
Scenery of Mount Lu

池、东林寺、白鹿洞书院、庐山植物园、庐山博物院等。牯岭镇是庐山上一座奇特的山城，也是庐山风景名胜区的游览中心。

庐山不但拥有"秀甲天下"的自然风光，更有着丰厚灿烂的文化内涵，是一座集风景、文化、教育为一体的千古名山。中国田园诗的开创者陶渊明就是庐山人。古往今来，无数文人墨客慕名登临庐山，为其留下4000余首诗词歌赋。晋代高僧慧远（334—416）在山中建立东林寺，并创了佛教中的"净土宗"，使庐山成为中国重要的宗教圣地。遗存至今的白鹿洞书院是中

highest Hanyang Peak is 1,474 meters above sea level. In the scenic area of 302 square kilometers, there are 171 peaks named in the ancient times, below which scatter 26 ridges, 20 gorges, 16 caverns and 22 grotesque rock sites. Watercourse splits and becomes narrow at the valley riverbed forming many rapids and waterfalls. This natural characteristic brought about 22 waterfalls, 18 creeks and 14 lakes in Mount Lu. The most famous Three Tiered Waterfall (*Sandie Quan*) has a drop of 155 meters. Other scenic spots include Five Elderly Men Peaks (*Wulao Feng*), *Hanpo* Pass, *Luling* Lake, Big Heavenly Pool (*Datian Chi*), Flower Path (*Huajin*), *Ruqin* Lake,

国古代教育和理学的重要学府。

　　庐山上还荟萃了各种风格迥异的建筑杰作。包括罗马式与哥特式的教堂、融合东西方艺术形式的拜

• 《匡庐图》（明 唐伯虎）
Painting of Kuanglu by Tang Bohu, Tang Dynasty (618-907)

Jinxiu Valley, Immortal Caves (*Xianren Dong*), Small Heavenly Pool (*Xiaotian Chi*), *Donglin* Temple, White Deer Cave Academy (*Bailudong Shuyuan*), Mount Lu Botanical Garden, Mount Lu Museum, etc. The tourist center of the Mount Lu's scenic area is Guling Town, a peculiar mountain village.

　　Mount Lu not only has the most striking scenery in the world, but also a famous mountain that unites natural beauty, culture, religion, education and politics into a coherent composition. It is the hometown of the Chinese pastoral poetry pioneer Tao Yuanming. It attracted numerous, scholars, artists and writers leaving behind about 4,000 poems and literary works. The Chinese Buddhist monk Huiyuan (334-416) of the Jin Dynasty founded the *Donglin* Temple on Mount Lu and started the Pure Land Buddhism making Mount Lu an important religious sacred site in China. The White Deer Cave Academy was once an important academy of Chinese ancient education and Neo-Confucianism.

　　There are different styles of architectures on the Mount Lu including Romanesque and Gothic churches, Byzantine architecture which is the fusion of Eastern and Western art forms,

占庭式建筑，以及日本式建筑和伊斯兰教清真寺等，堪称庐山风景名胜区的精华。

东林寺

东林寺坐落于庐山西麓，是晋代佛教大师慧远于东晋太元九年（384年）创建的，距今1600多年。东林寺橡摩栋接，丹辉碧映，是中国佛教八大道场之一。唐代，东林寺盛极一时，"殿、厢、塔、庑，共三百一十余间，规模宏远，足称万僧之居。"在历史上，东林寺对于中尼、中印、中日的文化交流与友好往来曾作出了重要贡献。经过1600多年的洗礼，东林寺屡建屡废，现存建筑主要有大雄宝殿、罗汉堂、玉佛殿（藏经楼）、祖师殿

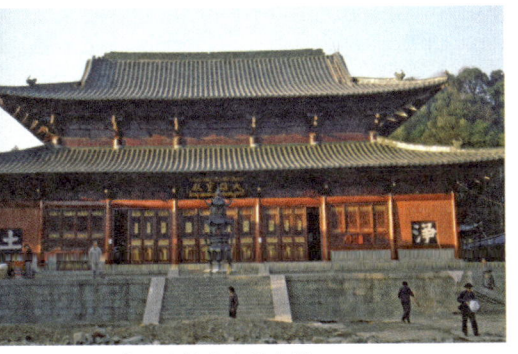

- 庐山东林寺大雄宝殿（图片提供：FOTOE）
Mahavira Hall in Mount Lu

Donglin Temple

Donglin Temple, located at the western foot of Mount Lu, was founded by Huiyuan, a Buddhist master of the Jin Dynasty in the year 384 about 1600 years ago. The *Donglin* Temple is one of the eight Buddhist sacred sites in China having multiple halls built with huge beams and painted in the contrasting colors of red and green. The temple became very prosperous during the Tang Dynasty (618-907) with a total 310 rooms, including different types of buildings such as halls and towers. It was known to have the capacity of housing over 10,000 monks. Monk Jianzhen (688-763) of the Tang Dynasty made several trips to Japan for the mission of preaching Buddhism. The *Donglin* Temple made contributions to improve cultural exchanges and friendly visits between China and Nepal, India, Japan. Over the course of 1,600 years, this temple was destroyed and rebuilt many times. The extant halls include Mahavira Hall (*Daxiong Baodian*), Arhat Hall

滕王阁

滕王阁位于江西省南昌市，与湖北黄鹤楼、湖南岳阳楼并称为"江南三大名楼"。滕王阁始建于唐永徽四年（653年），是古代收藏经史典籍的地方，许多士大夫迎送和宴请宾客也多喜欢在此设宴。这座阁楼主体建筑高57.5米，共7层，下部有象征古城墙的12米高台座。

Pavilion of Prince Teng (*Tengwang Ge*)

Pavilion of Prince Teng is located in Nanchang City, Jiangxi Province. It is equally famous with other two towers south of the Yangtze River. The other two are Yellow Crane Tower (*Huanghe Lou*) of Hubei Province and *Yueyang* Tower of Hunan Province. It was built in year 653 during the Tang Dynasty as a library for ancient history books. It also became a place where official scholars entertained their guests. The main structure is 57.5 meters high with seven stories on a 12-meter high platform representing ancient city walls.

● 滕王阁
Pavilion of Prince Teng

（三笑堂）、十八高贤殿（影堂）等。主殿是大雄宝殿，殿中供奉三世佛像。寺内文物众多，大文豪陶渊明、唐太宗李世民、鉴真大师等历史名人都曾在此留下过足迹。

三叠泉

庐山的水系发达，共形成了20多处大小瀑布，有"匡庐瀑布天下

(*Luohan Tang*), Jade Buddha hall (*Yufo Tang*) which is a library of Buddhist scriptures, Ancestors Hall (*Zushi Dian* or *Sanxiao Tang*), Hall of Eighteen Virtuous Men (*Ying Tang*), etc. The Mahavira Hall houses statues of three generations of Buddha. There are many relics in the temple including works of literary giant Tao Yuanming, Emperor Taizong of Tang Dynasty and Master Jianzhen.

奇"之美誉。三叠泉是庐山著名瀑布之一，位于五老峰下部，飞瀑流经的峭壁有三级，溪水分三叠飞泻而下，落差达155米，极为壮观，撼人魂魄。三叠泉每叠各具特色。一叠直垂，水从20多米的巅萁背上一倾而下；二叠弯曲，直入潭中，"上级如飘雪拖练，中级如碎玉摧冰，下级如玉龙走潭"；站在第三叠抬头仰望，三叠泉抛珠溅玉，宛如白鹭千羽，上下争飞。如果是暮

- 庐山三叠泉
  Three Tiered Waterfall in Mount Lu

Three Tiered Waterfall
(*Sandie Quan*)

Mount Lu has abundant water rasources, which forms over 20 big and small waterfalls. It is said that *Kuanglu* Waterfall is a wonder in the world. The Three Tiered Waterfall is one of the famous waterfalls in Mount Lu located below the Five Elderly Men Peak. The waterfall descends vertically into three tiers of steep rocks making the total drop of 155 meters. The view is spectacular and dramatic. Every tier has its own characteristics. In the first tier the waterfall has a vertical drop of more than 20 meters over the ridge. In the second tier the waterfall flows through twisting and narrow waterways into a deep pond with a scene described as a "flying snow chain on the top, broken jade pieces breaking the ice in the middle and jade dragon diving into the deep pond at the bottom". When standing at the third tier looking up, one can see thousands of water drops falling down as if the waterfall was splashing pearls and jade beads up and down like flying white egrets. The raining season between late spring and early summer witnesses the waterfall like an angry dragon rushing to the sky with a thunderous roar, making the sence breathtaking.

• 白鹿洞书院

白鹿洞书院位于庐山五老峰南麓，享有"海内第一书院"之誉。此书院始建于南唐升元年间，后来宋代理学家朱熹重建书院，亲自讲学，并奏请赐额及御书。从此，书院名声大振，成为古代中国的一个重要的文化摇篮。

White Deer Cave Academy

The White Deer Cave Academy at the southern foot of Five Elderly Men Peak once enjoyed a fame of "No. 1 academy in four seas". It was first built in year 940 during the Tang Dynasty and later expanded by Zhu Xi, the leading scholar of Neo-Confucianism in the Song Dynasty (960-1279). Zhu Xi personally came here to teach and petitioned for funding and imperial books from the emperor. From then on, the academy became a famous and an important cradle of culture in ancient China.

春初夏的多雨季节，飞瀑便如发怒的玉龙，冲破青天，凌空飞下，如雷声轰鸣，令人叹为观止。

不过，三叠泉长期隐藏在荒山深壑中。历史上曾隐居在其上源屏风叠的李白、在其下游白鹿洞讲学的朱熹都没发现它。

However the Three Tiered Waterfall was hiding in the deep mountain for a long time. Even Li Bai who once lived at the upper tier and Zhu Xi who was teaching at the White Deer Cave Academy at the lower tier did not know about the waterfall.

庐山云雾茶

庐山云雾茶是中国历史上十大名茶之一，主要茶区分布在海拔800米以上的含鄱口、五老峰、汉阳峰、小天池、仙人洞等地，以五老峰与汉阳峰之间所产的茶品质最佳。由于气候条件的原因，庐山云雾茶一般在谷雨后至立夏之间开始采摘，且每道工序都有严格要求，如杀青要保持叶色翠绿；揉捻要用手工轻揉，防止断碎；翻炒动作要轻，从而保证庐山云雾茶的品质。庐山云雾茶芽壮叶肥，幽香如兰，鲜爽甘醇。

Cloud Tea of Mount Lu

The Cloud Tea of Mount Lu is one of the ten famous tea types in the Chinese history. It is produced mainly in the areas 800 meters above sea level such as *Hanpo* pass, the Five Elderly Men Peak, *Hanyang* Peak, Small Heavenly Pool and Celestial Cave. Tea picked in the Five Elderly Men Peak and Hanyang Peak is considered the best. Because of the weather conditions of Mount Lu, tea leaves are picked between Grain Rain (the 20th day of the fourth month of Chinese Lunar Calender) and Beginning of Summer (the 6th day of the fifth month of Chinese Lunar Calender). Tea leaves are processed in very tedious and strict steps to ensure the high quality. For example, fixation is to maintain the green color of the tea leaves; tea leaves must be kneaded by hands to prevent tea leaves from breaking into small pieces; stiring and frying must be gentle to ensure the quality of tea. The Cloud Tea has bigger tea buds and thicker tea leaves having a fresh taste and a strong aroma similar to orchid fragrance.

• 庐山云雾茶
Cloud Tea of Mount Lu

美庐别墅

美庐别墅位于庐山牯岭东谷，掩隐在一片绿荫深处，是庐山特有的一处人文景观。美庐别墅始建

Meilu Villa

Meilu Villa is hidden in a green vegetation to the east of the *Guling* valley. It is an attraction of historical and cultural characteristics. It was built in 1903 by

于1903年，由英国兰诺兹勋爵建造，曾是蒋介石的夏都官邸，它展现了风云变幻的中国现代史的一个侧面，抗战时期的很多重大历史事件都在此研究决策。现今的"美庐别墅"已被辟为展览厅，其间留存物品包括陈列品、工艺品，亦有器皿、生活用品等，既反映出别墅主人生活的不同侧面，也体现出历史的真实。

the British Lord Lannoze and was once the official summer residence for Jiang Jieshi. During the War of Resistance against Japanese Aggression, many decisions on historical events took place here, reflecting one aspect of the modern history of China. Today *Meilu* Villa is opened up as an exhibition hall with arts, crafts, and utensils. It shows lives of its past residents and the reality of the history.

- **美庐别墅**

美庐别墅为石木结构，主楼为两层，附楼为一层，占地面积为455平方米。

Meilu Villa

Meilu Villa has a two-story main building and a one-story supplementary building with a total area of 455 square meters. The buildings are structures of wood and stone.

庐山与名人

庐山不仅以风景闻名于世，其浓厚的政治色彩也在中国的现当代史上留下了浓墨重彩的一笔。蒋介石就对庐山情有独钟，曾经三上庐山，并将庐山定为避暑的"夏都"。毛泽东也曾经三顾庐山。

Mount Lu and Famous Person

Mount Lu is not only well-known for its scenic beauty, but also strong political overtones in the modern history of China. It was a favorite place for Jiang Jieshi, who came to Mount Lu three times and made it his "summer residence". Mao Zedong also visited Mount Lu three times.

望庐山瀑布（唐 李白）

日照香炉生紫烟，遥看瀑布挂前川。
飞流直下三千尺，疑是银河落九天。

诗词译文：

香炉峰在阳光的照射下生起紫色的烟霞，远远望见瀑布好似白色绢绸悬挂在山前。高崖上飞腾直落的瀑布好像有三千尺，让人恍惚以为银河从天上泻落到人间。

***Watching Waterfalls of Lu Shan* by Li Bai, Tang Dynasty (618-907)**

Poem Interpretation

The Incense Summit glows in purple smoky clouds under the sunlight;
From afar the waterfall hangs over the mountain ridge like a white shimmering silk curtain;
Flying and dashing down three thousand feet from the high cliff,
As if the Milky Way fell from heaven to earth.

> 东南第一山——雁荡山

雁荡山位于浙江省东南部,乐清市境内,东起方岩顶,西至锯板岭,南起筋竹涧口,北达六坪山。雁荡山古名"芙蓉山",后因雁湖岗顶上有一个湖,芦苇众多,成了每年秋雁南飞的栖息地,于是在唐初时期改名"雁荡山",也称"雁山"。雁荡山山水形胜,以峰、瀑、洞、嶂见长,以山川奇秀而闻名天下,素有"寰中绝胜""海上名山"之誉,史称"东南第一山"。

雁荡山面积为450平方公里,境内有一百零二峰、六十四岩、四十六洞、二十八潭、十八瀑、十四嶂、十三坑,主峰百岗尖,海拔1056米。山中草木葱郁,群峰峥嵘,溪清潭碧,洞幽瀑奇,实为人

> No. 1 Mountain in Southeast China: Mount Yandang (*Yandang Shan*)

Mount Yandang is located in Yueqing City, southeast of Zhejiang Province. It starts from Square Rock Summit (*Fangyan Ding*) to the east, Sawing Board Ridge (*Juban Ling*) to the west, Hard Bamboo Stream Pass (*Jinzhu Jiankou*) to the south and Six Plains Mountain (*Liuping Shan*) to the north. It was called Mount Hibiscus (*Furong Shan*) in ancient times. In early Tang Dynasty, the name was changed to Mount Yandang or Mount Yan (Mount Wild Geese). Because a lake which growed lots of reeds was on top of Wild Geese Lake Ridge (*Yanhu Gang*), it became a habitat for migrating wild geese on their way to the south every year. Mount Yandang is characterized with stunning landscape of mountain peaks, waterfalls,

《十六罗汉·诺距罗》（唐 贯休）
Nakula, one of the sixteen Arhats by Guan Xiu, Tang (618-907) Dynasty

caves and steep cliffs. Its natural scenic wonders made a name for Mount Yandang as "the best in the vastness", "the famous mountain over the sea" and known to history as "the No. 1 mountain in the southeast".

Mount Yandang covers an area of 450 square kilometers, which comprises one hundred and two peaks, sixty-four rock sites, forty-six caves, twenty-eight pools, eighteen waterfalls, fourteen cliffs and thirteen ravines. The main peak A Hundred Ridge Summit (*Baigang Jian*) is 1,150 meter above sea level. It is considered as a scenic wonder on earth with lush greens, magnificent mountain peaks, clear ponds and streams, secluded caves and striking waterfalls.

Long history invested Mount Yandang abundant cultural connotations. It is said that Nakula, a disciple of Sakyamuni and also No. 5 of the sixteen Arhats, led three hundred of his pupils to build a temple in Mount Yandang. He died in a seated posture in front of the Big Dragon Waterfall (*Dalong Qiu*). Later he was respected as the ancestor to blaze the trails in Mount Yandang. Mount Yandang is embellished with Buddhist and Taoist temples. Almost every peak and rock has a Buddhist or immortal legend. Over

间胜景。

悠久的历史赋予了雁荡山丰厚的文化底蕴，据说如来佛的弟子、十六罗汉中排位第五的诺距罗曾率领三百弟子进山兴建寺院，后来在大龙湫观瀑坐化，于是后人奉他为

● 雁荡山风光 (图片提供：全景正片)
Scenery of Mount Yandang

雁荡的开山祖师。山上遍布佛寺、道观，就连一峰一石都拥有关于佛、仙的传说。千百年来，历代文士名流都在雁荡山留下了自己的足迹，景区内摩崖碑刻多达300余处，为名山锦上添花。

灵峰

灵峰是雁荡山的东大门，与灵岩、大龙湫并称"雁荡三绝"。灵峰景区东至蒲溪，南至白溪，北至马家岭，面积46平方公里。它以悬崖叠嶂、奇峰怪石、古怪石室、碧潭清润而著称，有二十六峰、三嶂、十八洞、三瀑、三十四岩、五石、五泉、四寺、二庵、七亭、四

thousands of years, many noted literati and figures in different dynasties left a large amount of literary works. Inside the scenic area there are over 300 rock and cliff inscriptions. It adds brilliance to its present splendor.

Spiritual Peak (*Ling Feng*)

Spiritual Peak (*Ling Feng*) serves as the east gate for Mount Yandang. It is one of the three scenic wonders together with the Spiritual Rock site (*Ling Yan*), and the Big Dragon Pool Waterfall (*Dalong Qiu*). It covers an area of 46 square kilometers extending east to the Sedge Creek (*Pu Xi*), south to the White Creek (*Bai Xi*), and north to the Ma Family Ridge (*Majia Ling*). Its scenery features

桥、二坊等131个景点。景区内层峦叠嶂,奇峰环拱,千形万状,美不胜收。两大奇洞——观音洞隐于合掌峰中,洞高113米,深76米,宽14米,洞中建有九层楼阁,为雁荡山第一洞天;北斗洞与伏虎峰遥遥相对,洞内高大宽敞,并建有凌霄殿,为雁荡山上最大道教洞天。白日里,灵峰上峰峦叠翠,风景宜人;而到了夜晚,这些奇峰异洞,

● 雁荡山灵峰 (图片提供:FOTOE)
Spiritual Peak in Mount Yandang

steep cliffs, layers of ridges, grotesque rocks and peaks, peculiar stone caves and clear ponds. It has a total of 131 scenic spots including twenty-six peaks, three ridges, eighteen caves, three waterfalls, thirty-four cliffs, five rock sites, five springs, four temples, two Buddhist convents, seven pavilions, four bridges and two memorial archways. Layers of mountain ridges with thousands of strangely shaped peaks and rocks unfold a breathtaking view. Hidden inside of the Holding Palms Peak (*Hezhang Feng*) is one of the two most amazing caverns in Mount Yandang: the Bodhisattva Guanyin Cavern (*Guanyin Dong*) which is 113 meters high, 14 meters wide and 76 meters deep. This cavern with a nine-story wooden hall built inside is called the "No. 1 Celestial Residence" in Mount Yandang. Opposite the Crouching Tiger Peak (*Fuhu Feng*) is the

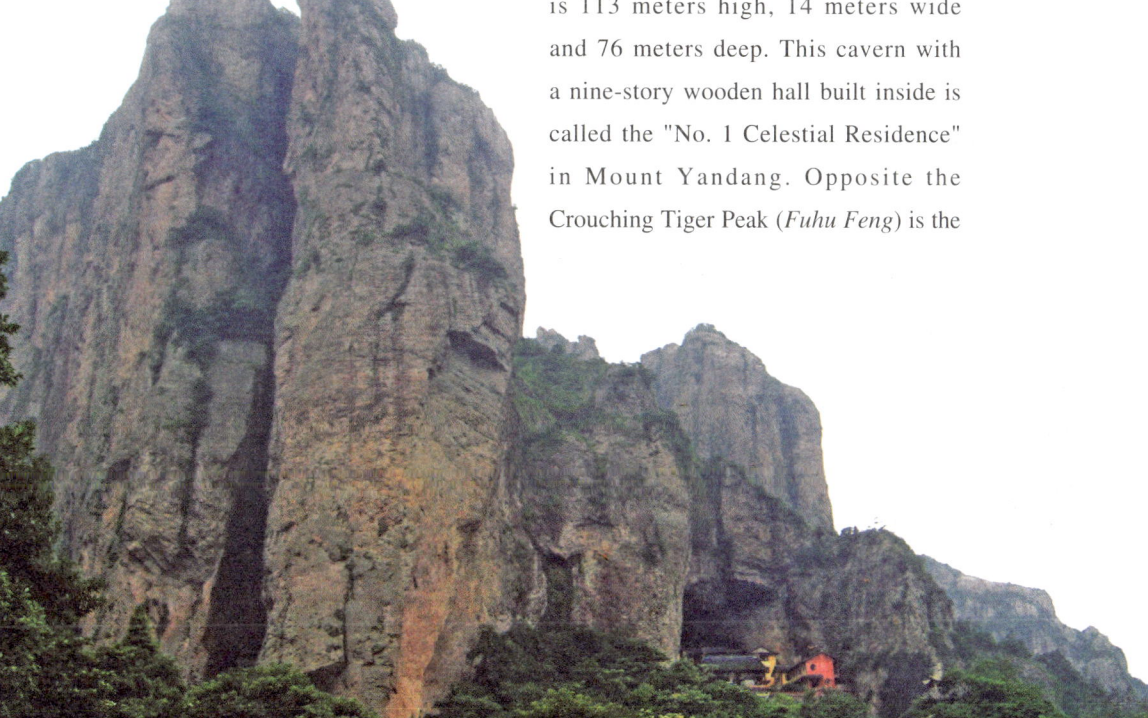

在朦胧的月色下又展现出更为绝妙、神秘的美景，随着月亮位置的变化，这些山峰屡屡变幻身姿，幻化出无数的美景，是雁荡山闻名于世的绝景之一。

灵岩

雁荡山之美以灵岩为第一。灵岩景区居雁荡山中心，东起响岩门，西至马鞍岭，南到飞泉寺，北达百岗尖，面积9平方公里。灵岩以灵岩古刹为中心，后有灿若云锦、极其形似的屏霞嶂，左右有雄伟高耸、拔地而起的天柱峰，紧紧相邻壮丽的展旗峰，天窗洞、龙

• 雁荡山灵岩景区的纱帽峰 (图片提供：FOTOE)
Imperial Official Cap Peak (*Shamao Feng*) in Mount Yandang

other amazing cavern, the spacious Big Dipper Cavern (*Beidou Dong*), which houses the Heavenly Hall (*Lingxiao Dian*) considered the biggest Taoist site for immortals in Mount Yandang. The Spiritual Peak displays a stunning scenery during the day. Under the misty moonlight, a mood of quietness and mystery prevails in these peculiar peaks and caves. The mountain peaks display a fantasy of their ever-changing postures known as one of the best scenery of Mount Yandang.

Spiritual Rocks (*Ling Yan*)

The Spiritual Rock site is acclaimed the No. 1 scenic beauty in Mount Yandang. It is right in the middle of the Yandang Mountain range starting from the Echo Rock Gate (*Xiangyan Meng*) in the east to Saddle Ridge (*Ma'an Ling*) in the west, Flying Spring Temple (*Feiquan Si*) in the south and Hundred Hillock Summit (*Baigang Jian*) in the north covering an area of

鼻水、小龙湫、玉女峰、双珠瀑巧妙融于峰峦沟壑之中，为雄壮的灵岩增添了灵动之美。整个景区群山环抱，峰峦之大气，古洞之诡怪，奇石之奇幻，溪瀑之秀美犹如天赐仙境。

大龙湫

大龙湫景区位于雁荡山中部偏西，东起马鞍岭，西至东岭，南起筋竹涧口，北至凌云尖。大龙湫境内峰奇洞异，崇岩叠嶂，飞瀑流泉，茂林幽谷。高耸天际的芙蓉峰，变化无穷的剪刀峰，云雨漠漠的经行峡，谷幽潭深的筋竹涧都堪称人间胜景。

被誉为"天下第一瀑"的大龙湫，变幻多姿，历代文人墨客，无不为大龙湫倾倒。大龙湫瀑布位于谷底连云嶂，水从卷壁中凌空腾飞而下，落差197米，为中国瀑布之最，有"天下第一瀑"之誉。大龙湫在半空中猛扑而下，如同一条发怒的银龙直捣潭心，声音振聋发聩，气势如虹。特别是在阳光的照射下，五色彩虹若隐若现，为大龙湫瀑布增添了一抹神秘而柔美的光环。

nine square kilometers. The focal point of the Spiritual Rock site is the ancient Spiritual Rock Temple with its back against the colorful Afterglow Screen Cliff (*Pingxia Zhang*), sided left and right by the abruptly rising Celestial Pillar Peak (*Tianzhu Feng*) and closely neighbored by the magnificent Fluttering Flag Peak (*Zhanqi Feng*). Layers of gorges and gullies are ingeniously blended with the Skylight Cave (*Tianchuan Dong*), Dragon Nose Spring (*Longbi Shui*), Small Dragon Pool Waterfall (*Xiaolong Qiu*), Fairy Peak (*Yunu Feng*) and Double Pearl Waterfall (*Shuangzhu Pu*) making even more vivid for the majestic Spiritual Rocks. This entire scenic site is a wonderland embraced by mountain ridges. Grand peaks, mysterious ancient caves, peculiar rocks and beautiful streams and waterfalls make Mount Yandang a good-given wonderland.

Big Dragon Pool Waterfall (*Dalong Qiu*)

Big Dragon Pool Waterfall (*Dalong Qiu*) is situated in the mid-west of Mount Yandang starting from the Saddle Ridge (*Ma'an Ling*) in the east to the East Ridge (*Dong Ling*) in the west, Hard Bamboo Streams (*Jinzhu Jian*) in the south and the

Soaring Cloud Summit (*Lingyun Jian*) in the north. The picturesque scenery of Big Dragon Pool Waterfall features peculiar peaks and caves, layers of cliffs and rocks, flying waterfalls and flowing streams, lush green forests and silent valleys. The most enthralling scenic spots include the Hibiscus Peak (*Furong feng*) soaring to the sky, the endlessly changing Scissors Peak (*Jiandao Feng*), the Walking Canyon (*Jingxing Xia*) always in misty rain and the Hard Bamboo Streams (*Jinzhu Jian*) in the deep, quiet valley.

Praised as the "No. 1 Waterfall in the World", the scenery of the Big Dragon Pool Waterfall undergoes constant and infinite transformation admired by writers and scholars in different dynasties. Over the Connecting to the Heaven Cliff (*Lianyun Zhang*), the Big Dragon Pool Waterfall shoots right out of curving cliffs to the sky and rushes straight down resulting a fall of 197 meters, the greatest of all waterfalls in China. It is described as a raging silver dragon storming right into the center of the deep pool with a huge roar and momentum. When the sun shines on the water, a colorful rainbow appears, sometimes hidden and sometimes visible giving mysterious splendor to the Big Dragon Pool Waterfall.

• 大龙湫瀑布 (图片提供：FOTOE)
Big Dragon Pool Waterfall

犀牛望月的传说

雁荡山上有一个犀牛峰，好似一只犀牛蹲在山峰上，仰头望月。关于犀牛峰，民间有一个美丽的传说。相传，古代有一位漂亮的年轻姑娘名叫玉贞，她从小就给土财主花老财当牧童，与牛同吃同住，相依为命。后来花老财看上了玉贞，欲占为己有。就在危急时刻，老牛大显神威，帮她逃离了财主。原来，这头牛是下凡的神仙。当他们跑到凌霞山时，发现没有了退路。这时，老牛突然开口说话了："我变成石头，把你送上月宫！"于是，玉贞随着一只牛角飞上天去了，而这只神牛就变成了独角的石头。

The Legend of the Rhinocer Looking at the Moon

The Rhinoceros Peak (*Xi'niu Feng*) on Mount Yandang looks like a rhino crouching at the mountain peak looking up to the moon. According to a beautiful folktale, a pretty young girl named Yuzhen was herding cattle for a rich old man called Hua Laocai. She lived together with the cattle and depended on each other for survival. The old man Hua tried to force her for himself. At this critical moment the cattle showed his magic and helped her run away from Hua Laocai. It turned out that the cattle was a deity coming down to earth from heaven. When they run to the Lingxia Peak and found no way out, the old cattle suddenly spoke to her, "let me turn into a rock and send you to the moon palace." Yuzhen rode on a cattle horn and flew to heaven. The old cattle became a horn-shaped rock.

● 雁荡山犀牛峰 (图片提供：FOTOE)
Rhinocer Peak in Mount Yandang

大龙湫（节选）（宋 楼钥）

一来气象不大侔，石屏倚天惊鬼设。

飞泉直自天际来，来处益高声益烈。

溟池倒泻三峡流，到此谁能定优劣？

雁山佳趣得要领，一日尽游神恶亵。

骊龙高卧唤不应，自愧笔端无电掣。

轮囷萧索湍不怒，非雾非烟亦非雪。

我闻冻雨初霁时，喷击生风散空阔。

更期雨后再来看，净洗一生烦恼热。

诗词译文：

这里的风景简直无法形容，倚天的石壁真可谓鬼斧神工。

飞流直下好似来自天际，落差愈大水声愈加喧闹。

这水如同天池倾泻，如同从三峡流出，水势湍急，无从分辨其优劣。

雁荡山的山水情趣要好好领略，一日尽游，那是对山神的轻慢。

眼前的大龙湫像黑龙高卧不动声色，我自愧无法用手中的笔唤醒它，令它风驰电掣。

此时的水流并不汹涌，仅仅是沿着岩壁弯曲而下，飞沫四溅，不像烟，不像雾，不像雪。

不过我听说，如果是暴雨初晴，这大龙湫就要奔腾咆哮，撞击岩石，挟着呼啸的风声向四处喷射。

我多么期望雨后可以再来观赏，用那汹涌的瀑布卷起的凉风，洗净烦恼和燥热。

***Big Dragon Pool Waterfall* by Lou Yao, Song Dynasty (1368-1644)**

Poem Interpretation

The scenery here is indescribable, sheer cliffs leaned against the sky as if they were the works of the divinities;

The water was pouring down from the celestial lake, the bigger the waterfall the louder the sound;

As the water was rushing out from the Three Gorges, at the place who can distinguish the virtue and vice of the turbulent rapids?

Take time to appreciate the beauty of Mount Yandang, one-day visit dishonors the god of mountain;

The Big Dragon Pool Waterfall before my eyes crouches like a quite dark dragon making me feel humbled to awake him and order him to dash out with my writing brush;

The water at the moment flows down the twists and turns of steep cliffs splashing everywhere, different from mist, fog or snow;

But I heard right after a storm the Big Dragon Waterfall will roar straight down beating cliffy rocks, and splashing with whistling wind;

How I wished I could come after the rain to watch the turbulent waterfall generating refreshing breeze to blow away all my worries and torridness.

- 《雁荡山图》（明 叶澄）
  Painting of Mount Yandang by Ye Cheng, Ming Dynasty (1368-1644)

> 东岳泰山

泰山自古以来就是中华文明的发祥地之一，也是孔孟儒家的发源地。几千年来，先后有12位皇帝来到泰山举行封禅祭拜大典，有94位帝王来此举行各种级别的参拜，故为"国之首山"，被称为"东岳大帝泰山神"。

泰山古称"岱宗""东岳"，是"五岳"之首，中国十大名山之一。泰山位于山东省东部，华北大平原的东侧，面积426平方公里，主峰海拔1545米，以其雄伟高大的自然景观、源远流长的精神文化和不胜枚举的人文景观闻名于世。泰山景色素以壮美著称，呈现出雄、奇、险、秀、幽、奥、旷等特点，被誉为"天下第一山"。沿山而上，山峰高耸入云，崖壁陡峭如

> East Sacred Mountain: Mount Tai (*Tai Shan*)

Mount Tai has always been considered the birthplace of the Chinese civilization and of Confucius and Mencius schools since ancient times. For thousands of years, twelve emperors came to Mount Tai to perform grand sacrifice rituals (*Fengshan*). Kings and emperors of ninety-four dynasties held different levels of ceremonies to pay homage to Mount Tai, which was respected as the "First Mountain of the Kingdom" and also known as the "Mount Tai God of the East Sacred Mountain".

Once named *Daizong* and *Dongyue* in ancient times, Mount Tai ranks the first of the five sacred mountains, and is one of the ten most famous mountains in China. It is situated in the eastern part of Shandong Province, at the east side of the North China Plain. It covers an area of

削，密密匝匝的台阶如同通天之梯一般；盘踞在崖峰谷底的山石如龙如虎、惟妙惟肖；潺潺不息的流水在林木石岩之间若隐若现，苍劲的松柏在这块土地上恣意生长，这些景色和谐共融，组成了众多引人入胜的景观。

426 square kilometers, and the average altitude of Mount Tai is 1,545 meters. Mount Tai is famous for its magnificent natural landscape, a long history of spiritual culture as well as innumerable sites of cultural heritage. Its scenic beauty is described as grandeur, spectacular, steep, enchanting, serene, vast and unfathomable. It is hailed as the "First Mountain in the World". When climbing up, the scenery gradually unfolds towering mountain peaks, precipitous cliffs, and thousands of paved stairs as if they were the ladder to the sky; rocks crouching at the top of the mountain or in the valley resemble life-like tigers and dragons; streams flow through woods and ridges sometimes hidden and sometimes visible; ancient pines grow everywhere at will. Everything is in perfect harmony presenting an enchanting natural landscape wonder.

The majestic natural beauty of Mount Tai has attracted numerous notable Chinese artists and scholars. As early as the Spring and Autumn Period (770 B.C. -476 B.C.), Confucius said, "Only by ascending Mount Tai will you realize how small the world is." Since then, there were thousands of well-known quotations about Mount Tai in the following

• 泰山风光
Scenery of Mount Tai

• 泰山石刻

Stone Carving of Mount Tai

泰山雄浑壮丽的自然景观吸引了无数名人雅士登临游览。早在春秋时期，孔子就留下了"登泰山而小天下"的赞叹。此后数千年间，关于泰山的名句数以千计，司马迁的"人固有一死，或重于泰山，或轻于鸿毛"、杜甫的"会当凌绝顶，一览众山小"都为泰山冠上了雄伟、庄严的光环。泰山现存多处古遗址、古墓葬、古建筑、石窟造像，以及近现代文物12处、文物藏品万余件，尤其历代石刻多达2500余处，被誉为"中国摩崖石刻博物馆"。1987年，泰山被列入《世界自然文化遗产名录》。

thousands of years, such as "Though death befalls all men alike, it may be weightier than Mount Tai or lighter than a feather" by Sima Qian and "Climbing up to the top of mountain overlooking the scenery, all other seems like small mountains" by Du Fu. These famous quotes crown Mount Tai with an aura of solemnity and sublimity. At present, Mount Tai maintains several ancient ruins and tombs, ancient architectural complexes, and grotto statues in addition to 12 sites of modern cultural heritage, over ten thousand pieces of cultural relics and over 2,500 rock inscriptions of different dynasties. Mount Tai is also acclaimed the "Chinese Museum of Cliffside Inscriptions Carvings". Mount Tai became a UNESCO World Heritage Site in 1987.

- 泰山石刻
Stone Carving of Mount Tai

• 泰山天阶坊

天阶坊位于泰山红门宫前，额书"天阶"，高6米。

Heavenly Stairway Gate (*Tianjie Fang*) in Mount Tai

The six-meter high Heavenly Stairway Gate is located in front of the Mount Tai Red Gate Palace with a tablet inscription "Heavenly Stirway" (*Tianjie*).

盘古开天辟地的传说

相传在日月混沌、天地初分的时候,一个名叫盘古的巨人生活在这个空间里。盘古天生神力,每日长一丈。经过一万八千年的岁月,将天地开辟,成就了现在的世界。等盘古死后,他的左眼变成了太阳,右眼变成了月亮,头发和胡须变成了夜空的星星,身体变成了东、西、南、北四极和雄伟的三山五岳,血液变成了江河,牙齿、骨骼和骨髓变成了地下矿藏,皮肤和汗毛变成了大地上的草木,汗水变成了雨露,灵魂变成了人类。因此盘古被中国古人尊为人类的祖先,而他头部化成的泰山也被尊为五岳之首。

The Legend of Pangu Creating the Universe

It is said that in the prehistoric times there was no sky or earth except chaos embedded in a cosmic egg. A gigantic man named Pangu lived inside the egg. Possessing some magic power, Pangu grew ten feet high a day for eighteen thousand years and eventually separated the sky from the earth. The universe became the world today. After his death, his left eye became the sun and his right eye became the moon; his hair and beard turned into stars at night; his body formed the four peaks to bear the sky at all directions and the three great mountains and five sacred mountains; his blood turned into rivers; his teeth and bones changed to different underground minerals; his skin and fine hair became grass and woods on earth; his sweat fell as rain and morning dews; and his soul became mankind. Therefore, Pangu was respected by ancient Chinese as the ancestor of mankind. Mount Tai, which was said to transform from his head, was also regarded as the first of the five sacred mountains.

- 盘古开天辟地
  Pangu Creating the Universe

封禅

　　封禅是中国古代帝王为祭拜天地而举行的活动，"封"为"祭天"，"禅"为"祭地"。中国古代帝王为了加强自己的统治，宣传"君权天授"的理论，为了使这种理论得以证明，便有了封禅的活动。封禅仪式在中岳嵩山和东岳泰山都曾举行过，但以泰山的次数多且影响大。古人认为，群山之中以泰山最高，为"天下第一山"，因此人间的帝王应到此祭拜天地，才算受命于天。自秦始皇开始，至宋真宗止，共有六帝十次封禅泰山。

Fengshan

Fengshan refers to sacrifice ceremonies held by ancient Chinese emperors to pay homage to heaven and earth. *Feng* was the sacrifice for the heaven and *Shan* was the sacrifice for the earth. To strengthen their rule, ancient Chinese emperors advocated that their divine power was awarded by heaven and *Fengshan* were performed to prove this theory. These ceremonies took place in the Central Sacred Mountain Mount Song and the East Sacred Mountain Mount Tai, which the latter held more sacrifices and as a result was better known. It was a common belief of ancient Chinese that Mount Tai was the highest mountain and "the No. 1 Mountain in the World". Therefore emperors must come here to pay respect to heaven and earth to be accepted by heaven. From the first emperor of China in the Qin Dynasty to Emperor Zhenzong of the Song Dynasty, six emperors came to Mount Tai to conduct *Feng Shan* sacrifices ten times.

- 泰山自古以来就被尊为五岳之首
  Mount Tai is regarded as the first of the five sacred mountains since ancient times.

岱庙

岱庙又称"东岳庙",位于泰山脚下,是泰山最大的古建筑群,也是历代帝王举行封禅大典和祭祀泰山神的地方。岱庙始建于秦汉时期,宋代时曾扩修,是历代帝王的泰山行宫。历代帝王登封泰山前,都要在山下岱庙内举行大典,然后再登山。岱庙城墙高筑,庙貌巍峨,宫阙重叠,庙内各类古建筑有150余间。天贶殿是岱庙的主体建筑,为东岳大帝的神宫。殿内北、东和西三面墙壁上绘有巨幅《泰山

- 岱庙远观
  A Distance View of *Dai* Temple

Dai Temple

Dai Temple, also known as the East Sacred Mountain Temple, is situated at the foot of Mount Tai. It is the largest ancient building complex in Mount Tai and the place where emperors of different dynasties performed *Fengshan* and pay homage to the God of Mount Tai. *Dai* Temple was built during the Qin and Han dynasties and expanded in the Song Dynasty when it became the imperial palace for emperors. Before they ascended Mount Tai, emperors usually performed a grand ceremony in the *Dai* Temple at the foot of Mount Tai. Surrounded by high walls, the *Dai* Temple has a majestic appearance and multiple rows of imperial halls. There are over 150 various ancient building structures. Inside the complex, the centerpiece is the Hall of Heavenly Blessings (*Tiankuang Dian*). It is regarded as a celestial palace of the Great Eastern Mountain God. On the eastern, western and northern walls of the hall painted a huge mural called "The God of Mount Tai Making a Journey" depicting the glory and grandeur of an inspection tour by the God of Mount Tai.

• 岱庙天贶殿

天贶殿是岱庙的主体建筑，位于岱庙中轴线的中后部，始建于北宋，是泰山神东岳大帝的宫殿。

Hall of Heavenly Blessings(*Tiankuang Dian*) in *Dai* Temple

Hall of Heavenly Blessings is the main building in *Dai* Temple located along the central axis in the mid-rear part of the complex. It was built in the Northern Song Dynasty (960-1279) and considered the palace for the God of East Sacred Mountain.

神启跸回銮图》，描绘了泰山神出巡的浩荡壮观的场面。

天柱峰

天柱峰是泰山主峰之巅，又名"玉皇顶"，海拔1545米，气势雄伟，拔地而起，有"天下第一

Heavenly Pillar Peak (*Tianzhu Feng*)

The Heavenly Pillar Peak, also known as the "Yudi Summit" (*Yuhuang Ding*) is the highest main peak in Mount Tai at an elevation of 1,546 meters. Known as the "No. 1 Peak in the world", the magnificent peak rises from the ground and was named after the Yudi Temple (*Yuhuang Miao*) built on the summit. The temple houses a

• 玉皇庙
Yudi Temple

山峰"之美誉，因峰顶的玉皇庙而得名。殿内祀玉皇大帝铜像，神龛上匾额题"柴望遗风"，意思是远古帝王曾在这里燔柴祭天，祀拜山川诸神。玉皇顶上有一处"古登封台"碑刻，是历代帝王登封泰山时设坛祭天的地方。

bronze statue of the Yudi and a hanging tablet over his shrine inscribed "*Chaiwang Yifeng*" meaning that this place was once used for burning sacrifices with woods and ancient emperors paid homage to heaven and mountain deities. Another rock inscription on the peak also indicates that this was once the place where emperors of different dynasties came to set altar and offer sacrifices to heaven in Mount Tai.

泰山"四大奇观"
Four Scenic Worder in Mount Tai

旭日东升、晚霞夕照、黄河金带、云海玉盘被称为泰山"四大奇观"。

The four scenic wonders in Mount Tai are: Sunrise in the East, Sunset Glow, Golden Belt of the Yellow River and the Sea of Clouds.

旭日东升

泰山日出是泰山最动人心弦的景观之一。清晨时分，星辰寥寥，云海苍苍，泰山群峰在一片静谧之中沉睡着。天色慢慢亮了起来，天空中翳翳的云朵明亮起来，翻滚涌动，远处的山峰轮廓渐渐清晰分明。光线越来越强，如同水流一般将黑暗冲淡冲散。随着火红的旭日艰难地从天际露出一点头，发出的第一缕曙光终于穿透了云层，万道霞光惊醒了崇山峻岭。一时间，云在翻腾、树在伸展、鸟在鸣叫，嫣红的大地充满了勃勃生机！

Sunrise in the East

One of the most enthralling views in Mount Tai is the sunrise. At dawn when a few stars are visible in the sea of clouds, the mountain range is still deep in silence. The sky slowly lights up with clouds rolling and getting brighter. The increasingly bright light washes away the darkness like a flow of water and gradually reveals the mountain peak silhouette. The red rising sun moves slowly above the horizon and with its first stream of sunlight breaks through the clouds. Millions of glowing rays wake up the entire mountain range. All of sudden clouds are rolling, trees are stretching, birds are singing and the whole earth covered with bright red sunshine is full of vitality.

晚霞夕照

当倦鸟归巢、夕阳西下的时候，漫步泰山极顶，便仿佛置身于一片色彩绚烂的仙境之中。随着夕阳西下，晚霞如同水墨一般泼洒在泰山的云海和峰峦之间。随着夜晚的临近，晚霞渐渐与云雾融在一起，弥漫在遥远天际。

当雨过天晴、天高气爽、夕阳西下时，仰望西天，若云海恰在此时出现，满天的霞光便会映照在"大海"之中。待夕阳沉入云底，霞光变成了一片火红，天际、云朵、峰峦似在燃烧，色彩瑰丽动人，蔚为大观。

Sunset Glow

At the sunset when tiring birds fly back to their nests, the highest summit of Mount Tai is immersed with bright colors as if it was a fairyland. With the sun going down in the west, the sunset glow pours over the mountain peaks and the sea of clouds like an ink painting. When nightfall comes, the sunset glow slowly merges with misty clouds suffusing from the faraway horizon.

After a storm when the air is refreshing, if the sea of clouds appears, there will be a spectacle of sunset glow in the sky as if it is the sea in the sky". When the sun sets at the bottom of the clouds, the glow turns into fiery red as if the clouds, the peaks and the skyline were all set on fire burning in magnificent colors.

黄河金带

在秋高气爽、夕阳西下之际，在泰山顶上登高望远，层层峰峦如同小丘般簇拥着泰山。在西北处，黄河如同一条金光闪闪的飘带一般从西南向东北方向逶迤延伸，在落日余晖的照耀下灵动飘逸、波光粼粼，愈发映衬得泰山巍峨壮观。这个绚丽雄壮的景观便是"黄河金带"，清代诗人袁枚咏诗描绘如此美景："一条黄水似衣带，穿破世间通银河。"

Golden Belt of the Yellow River

In the fall Mount Tai enjoys nice weather and fresh air. Overlooking the sunset from the highest summit, one can see Mount Tai is surrounded by layers of peaks and ridges. In the northwest, the Yellow River extends from southwest to northeast winding like a golden belt floating and glittering under the sunset glow, making Mount Tai even more magnificent. This spectacle is called the "Golden Belt of the Yellow River" and described in a poem written by poet Yuan Mei in the Qing Dynasty as "a stream of yellow water like a clothing belt, flowing through the earth all the way to the Milky Way."

云海玉盘

夏天，雨后初晴，大量水蒸气上升，从海上吹来的暖温空气被高压气流控制在海拔1500米左右的高度时，就会幻化成云雾。在没有风的日子里，置身玉皇顶俯瞰群山，视线里层层叠叠的白云绵软祥和，如同浩瀚大海中一朵朵柔和的浪花，时而轻柔地包围着群峰，时而翻江倒海，冲击着坚毅的山岳。在天气晴朗的时候，远处的云如同玉带般轻轻系在山峦之间，灵秀飘逸；近处的云朵如同山谷积雪，一团团玉盘似的堆叠在你的手边，这就是著名的"云海玉盘"。

Sea of Clouds like Jade Plates
In the summer, a large amount of water vapor evaporates and rises up after a storm. When the warm air from the sea is kept by the high pressure at around 1,500 meters above sea level, it becomes misty clouds. In a windless day, the Yuhuang Peak displays a scenic beauty of overlapping calm white clouds as if they were spindrifts in the vast ocean sometimes embracing mountain peaks softly and sometimes overturning the sea hitting against the mountain cliffs. When the sky is clear, distant clouds float around mountain ridges as if they were ribbons tied on the mountain; clouds close by piled up in the valley like accumulated snow and like jade plates piled up on top near your hand, it is known as the wonder "the Sea of Clouds like Jade Plates".

• 泰山风光
Landscape of Mount Tai

望岳（唐 杜甫）

岱宗夫如何？齐鲁青未了。
造化钟神秀，阴阳割昏晓。
荡胸生层云，决眦入归鸟。
会当凌绝顶，一览众山小。

诗词译文：

　　五岳之首泰山的景象如何？在齐鲁大地上，那青翠的山色没有尽头。

　　大自然把神奇和秀美都赋予了泰山，它是天地间神秀之气的集中所在。

　　泰山巍峨高大，山南和山北被分割成一明一暗，犹如早晨和黄昏。

　　层层云霭雾气升腾，使我心胸激荡，凝神远望，目送山中的飞鸟归林。

　　登上泰山的顶峰，俯瞰群山，竟是如此渺小！

• 《泰山松图》（明 盛茂烨）
Painting: Pine Trees of Mount Tai by Sheng Maoye, Ming Dynasty (1368-1644)

View of Mountain by Du Fu, Tang Dynasty (618-907)

Poem Interpretation

How is the view on Mount Tai?

The land of Qi Lu (today's Shandong Province) sees endless green mountains;

Nature gives all magical and elegant beauty to Mount Tai capturing spirits of heaven and earth on itself;

Magnificent Mount Tai is divided into north and south ridges, one bright and one dark resembling morning and dusk;

Misty clouds rise up layer upon layer stirring my heart and soul;

Looking into distance, I see birds off to return to the woods;

Overlooking from the top of Mount Tai, all mountains below seem small and insignificant.

> 中岳嵩山

嵩山位于河南省登封市西北面，东依省会郑州，西临古都洛阳，南依颍水，北邻黄河，面积450平方公里，东西绵延60多公里，是中华文明的发源地之一。嵩山古时曾称"外方""嵩高""崇高"。嵩山自然景观绚丽多姿、峻幽迷人，主要由东部的太室山与西部的

• 《崇山萧寺图》（明末清初 邹喆）
Buddhist Temple on Mount Song by Zou Jie, Late Ming and Early Qing Dynasty

> Central Sacred Mountain: Mount Song (*Song Shan*)

Mount Song (*Song Shan*) is situated in the northwest of Dengfeng City, Henan Province, neighboring the provincial capital Zhengzhou city to the east, ancient capital Luoyang city to the west, Ying River to the south and the Yellow River to the north. It covers an area of 450 square kilometers extending over 60 kilometers from east to the west. It is one of the birthplaces of Chinese civilization. Mount Song was called *Waifang*, *Songgao* and *Chonggao* in ancient times. Mount Song is well known for its colorful and enchanting natural landscape. It is made up of two mountain ranges, Mount Taishi (*Taishi Shan*) to the east and Mount Shaoshi (*Shaoshi Shan*) to the west, each with 36 peaks. Of the total 72 Mount Song peaks, the highest is the Connecting to Heaven Peak

● 嵩山风光 (图片提供：全景正片)
Scenery of Mount Song

少室山组成。太室山和少室山各有36峰，合称嵩山72峰，其中最高峰为少室山的连天峰，海拔1512米。嵩山林木苍郁，山峰连绵起伏，地势复杂，山谷、奇洞数不胜数，深

(*Liantian Feng*) in Mount Shaoshi at an altitude of 1,512 meters. Mount Song has dense forests, waves of mountain ridges, complex topography and numerous caves and valleys dotted with deep pools and waterfalls throughout. In Mount Tai, a

潭、银瀑点缀其间，险峻处一线连天，平坦处视野开阔。

作为最古老的山脉之一，嵩山拥有悠远的历史和厚重的文化底蕴，无数名胜古迹遍布山间，种种传说不胜枚举。这座古老的山脉具

precipitous place looks like a straight strip connecting to the sky and a flat terrace offers an open vista.

Mount Song, one of the most ancient mountain ranges in China, has a long history and deep cultural roots. It is full of historical sites and cultural relics associated with numerous legends. Mount Tai contains around 400 temples, monasteries and academy of classical learning bringing three different philosophies of Confucianism, Buddhism and Taoism into harmony. Many noted Taoist monks wrote books and gave lectures in the Central Mountain Temple (*Zhongyue Miao*) including the famous Indian monk Bodhidharma (Dharma in Chinese) who once retreated in the *Shaolin* Temple. Well-known thinkers and scholars Fan Zhongyan and Sima Guang taught in the Songyang Academy. Renowned literary figures such as calligrapher Yan Zhenqing and poet Su Dongpo left many celebrated poems, verses and calligraphy works for the later generations to enjoy and appreciate.

- 《达摩图》（明 吴彬）
Bodhidharma by Wu Bing, Ming Dynasty (1368-1644)

有深厚的文化底蕴，儒、佛、道三家融会贯通，现存庙宇、书院400余间。历代名道士曾在中岳著书讲道，印度名僧菩提达摩禅师曾驻锡少林寺，著名思想家范仲淹、司马光等在嵩阳书院桃李天下，颜真卿、苏东坡等文人雅士更是在山上留下无数名诗佳句、珍贵墨宝供后人品味赏析。

少林寺

少林寺坐落于嵩山腹地少室山下的茂密丛林中，始建于北魏太和十九年（495年），由孝文帝元宏为安顿印度僧人佛陀跋陀罗而依山辟基创建，是佛教禅宗祖庭和少林武术的发祥地。少林寺常住院总面积3万多平方米，为少林寺的核心建筑，是僧人进行佛事活动的地方。中轴线上有山门、天王殿、大雄宝殿等七进建筑，中轴线两侧有钟楼、鼓楼、六祖殿、文殊殿等附属建筑。少林寺以古老的佛教文化而闻名，北魏孝昌三年（527年），释迦牟尼的第二十八代佛徒菩提达摩历时三年到达少林寺，并在此创立了佛教中影响力最大的宗派——

Shaolin Temple

Located in the dense forests at the foot of Mount Shaoshi in the center of Mount Song, the *Shaolin* Temple was built in the Northern Wei Dynasty in year of 495 by Emperor Xiaowen in order to provide accommodation for Indian monk Buddhabhadra. It is the birthplace of both the *Chan* sect and *Shaolin* martial arts. The main structure in the temple is a residential complex of over 30,000 square meters, a place where monks perform their Buddhist functions. Along the central axis of the temple stand seven buildings including the temple gate, the Hall of Heavenly King (*Tianwang Dian*) and the Mahavira Hall (*Daxiong Baodian*). Subsidiary structures were built on both sides of the central axis including the Clock Tower (*Zhong Lou*), the Drum Tower (*Gu Lou*), the Sixth Ancestor Hall (*Liuzu Dian*) and Manjusri Hall (*Wenshu Dian*). *Shaolin* Temple is widely known for its ancient and mysterious Buddhist culture. Bodhidharma, the 29th generation of Sakyamuni disciples, went through three years of hardships to arrive here in the year of 527 in the Northern Wei Dynasty and founded the most influential *Chan* school of Buddhism. Therefore, the *Shaolin* Temple was once

禅宗。因此，少林寺被世界佛教界称为"禅宗祖庭"。唐朝时，少林寺鼎盛之极，博得了"天下第一名刹"的美誉。

现在的少林寺不仅因其古老的佛教文化名扬天下，更因其精湛的

called "the Ancestral Temple of the Zen Sect of Buddhism" by Buddhists around the world. Its fame culminated in the Tang Dynasty (618-907) and won the reputation as the "No. 1 Temple in the World."

Today's *Shaolin* Temple is not only well known for its ancient and mysterious Buddhist culture, but also for its world famous martial arts. There is a saying that "the Chinese martial arts are the best in the world and the best martial arts come from *Shaolin*". *Shaolin* Temple is the birthplace of *Shaolin Wushu* (martial arts), which, after 1500 years of perfection, traditions and

- 少林寺塔林 (图片提供：全景正片)

塔林位于少林寺西300米的山脚下，是自唐朝以来历代少林寺住持的墓地。塔林内有240多座塔，大小不等，形态各异，是中国最大的塔林。

Pagoda Forest in *Shaolin* Temple

Pagoda Forest, located at the foot of the mountain 300 meters west of *Shaolin* Temple, is the cemetery for *Shaolin* masters of different dynasties since the Tang Dynasty. It is the largest pagoda forest in China with over 250 pagodas of different sizes and forms.

少林功夫而驰名中外，有"中国功夫冠天下，天下武功出少林"的说法。这里是少林武术的发源地。历经1500年的锤炼、传承和发展，少林武术已经形成了一种独特的文化现象，是举世公认的中国武术正宗流派。

嵩阳书院

嵩阳书院，原名"嵩阳寺"，位于嵩山南麓、太室山下，是中国著名的儒教圣地，与河南的应天书院以及湖南的岳麓书院、江西的白鹿洞书院并称为"中国古代四大书院"。嵩阳书院始建于北魏太和八年（484年），北宋时期成为著名的教育场所，名儒范仲淹、程颐、程颢、司马光等人都曾在此讲学，是宋代理学的发源地之一。嵩阳书院历经元、明、清各代重修增建，鼎盛时期，生徒达数百人，藏书达1000多册。

嵩阳书院明末一度毁于兵火，清康熙十三年（1674年）重建。现在的建筑为清代规制，建筑保留完整，保存了传统书院的建筑格调。中轴线的主要建筑，从大门到藏书

development, has become a special kind of cultural phenomenon and an authentic school of Chinese martial arts recognized worldwide.

Songyang Academy

Songyang Academy, originally named *Songyang* Temple, is located at the foot of Mount Taishi, south of Mount Song. It is a famous sacred place of Confucianism and one of the four greatest ancient academies in China, the other three being *Yingtian* Academy of Henan Province, *Yuelu* Academy of Hunan Province and White Deer Cave Academy (*Bailu Shuyuan*) of Jianxi Province. *Songyang* Academy was founded in the year of 484 during the Northern Wei Dynasty and became a distinguished school of learning in the Northern Song Dynasty (960-1279). Noted scholars such as Fang Zhongyan, Cheng Yi, Cheng Hao and Sima Guang all lectured here. It was one of the birthplaces of Neo-Confucianism of the Song Dynasty. Songyang Academy was rebuilt and expanded respectively in the Yuan (1206-1368), Ming (1368-1644) and Qing (1616-1911) dynasties. During its most prosperous period, it had several hundred students and a collection of over 1000 books.

● 嵩阳书院 (图片提供: FOTOE)

嵩阳书院是中国古代四大书院之一，书院建制古朴雅致，环境幽美，是中国古代的高等学府。

Songyang Academy

Songyang Academy is one of the four greatest ancient academies in China. The academy has a classic and simply layout in a tranquil environment. It was a school of higher learning in ancient China.

楼，前后五进院落，最前为卷棚大门三间，正楹为先圣殿，次为讲堂，讲堂后为道统祠，最后为藏书楼。中轴线两侧配房，分别为程朱祠、丽泽堂、博学斋书舍等。整个书院建筑古朴典雅，巍然壮观。

The *Songyang* Academy was once destroyed in the war in the late Ming Dynasty and was rebuilt in 1674 during the Qing Dynasty. The extant structure is based on the Qing Dynasty building principles and retains the traditional architectural style. Main structures from the front gate to the sutras library are aligned with the central axis and divided into five courtyards. At the very front are three *Juanpeng* halls (halls that have a open walkway from the front to the back with no doors), followed by a memorial hall for ancestors (*Xiansheng Dian*), the lecture hall (*Jiang Tang*), a Confucian temple (*Daotong Ci*) and finally a library in the rear. On both sides of the central axis are *Chengzhu* Temple, *Lize* Hall and *Boxuezhai* Library. The entire building of the academy is simple, elegant and magnificent.

Astronomical Observatory (*Guanxing Tai*)

Situated to the north of Mount Song, the Astronomical Observatory is the oldest facility of its kind existing in China today, and a world famous building of astronomical science. The Astronomical Observatory of Mount Song was built between 1276 and 1279 during the

观星台

观星台北依嵩山，是中国现存最古老的天文台，世界上著名的天文科学建筑物。观星台创建于元朝至元十三年至十六年（1276—1279），距今已有740多年的历史，是保存完好的元代天文观测仪器。它是元代天文学家郭守敬进行"四海测验"（当时在中国范围内进行的一次规模空前的地理纬度测量活动）时，在中国所建的27个观测站

Yuan Dynasty with well-preserved astronomical observation instruments. It has a long history of over 740 years, and it is the only surviving observatory of the 27 ancient observatories built to conduct geographical latitude measuring activities unprecedented in China known as "four seas measurements" by Chinese astronomer Guo Shoujing of the Yuan Dynasty. There are seven structures including the front screen wall (*Zhaobi*), the front gate(*Shanmen*), the second entrance gate(*Chuihuamen*), Duke

● 观星台（图片提供：全景正片）
Astronomical Observation Terrace

的中心天文台之一，也是现今仅存的一处。观星台前后院落共分照壁、山门、垂花门、周公测影台、大殿、观星台、螽斯殿等七进，院内复制安装各种天文仪器十多种，主要功能是"昼参日影，夜观极星，以正朝夕"，就是通过观测日影长短和方向来确定节气，通过寻找日、月、星辰运动的规律，作为制订历法的依据。观星台反映了当时中国在天文学上的成就，不管在世界天文史上还是建筑史上都有重要的影响和研究价值。

Zhou's Gnomon (*Zhougong Ceying Tai*), the main hall (*Dadian*), Astronomical Observation Terrace (*Guanxing Tai*) and *Zhongsi* Hall. In the complex, dozens of astronomical measuring instruments were installed for the purpose of observing the length of the shadows casted by sun to decide on solar terms and the regular movements of the sun, the moon and the stars which were used as a basis to make calendars. The Astronomical Observatory reflects the astronomical achievements of China at that time, which had important research value and great impact on the world's history of astronomy and architecture.

启母石的传说

自大禹子承父业接受了治水的任务之后，殚精竭虑，励精图治。经过研究，他发现要治水，"导"胜于"堵"，于是他决定先凿开太室山。为能尽快完工，大禹化作黄熊，日夜不停地工作，连吃饭都是他的妻子送到山上来。大禹与妻子约定，以鼓声为暗号，当大禹饿了的时候，下山击鼓，妻子就送饭上来。但是有一次，山上的石块掉落下来，正巧击落在鼓上，发出声响，妻子以为大禹饿了，忙送饭上来，谁知道上山后没有看到自己的丈夫，却看到一只开山的黄熊。已身怀六甲的妻子惊慌失措，掉头就逃，在逃跑的过程中化作了一块岩石。大禹见此情景大喊一声："我的儿子！"只见一个婴儿从石缝中迸裂而出，就是后来的夏启，而妻子化成的那块石头也因此称作"启母石"。

Story of "Rock of Qi's Mother"

According to legend, Yu the Great (*Dayu*) built a system to control flooding. When he inherited his father's task to control flooding, Yu the Great exerted all his efforts and intelligence to design irrigation and dredging system. After some investigations, he realized that directing water overflow to other places would be more effective than building a dam to block the water. He decided to chisel through Mount Taishi. He transfigured into a yellow bear to work day and night so that he could finish the work as early as possible. His wife would bring food to him every day. They agreed that when he felt hungry, Yu the Great would beat the drum to signal his wife to bring food to him in the mountain. But once a rock fell and accidentally hit the drum, his wife thought it was time to send him some food. When she walked up the mountain she saw a big yellow bear instead of her husband. His pregnant wife became panic and ran away. While running away, she began to change into a big rock. Yu the Great shouted at her "My son!" and a baby burst out from the rock. The baby later became Xia Qi, the second ruler of the Xia Dynasty. The rock that his mother changed to was later named "Rock of Qi's Mother."

- 大禹治水
  Yu the Great Taming the Flood

> 南岳衡山

衡山，又名"岣嵝山"或"虎山"，是中国五岳之一，位于湖南省衡阳市南岳区，紧邻湘江，主峰海拔1300米，具有"五岳独秀"的美誉。衡山是一座花岗岩断块山，

衡山远眺（图片提供：FOTOE）
Overlooking from Mount Heng

> South Sacred Mountain: Mount Heng (*Heng Shan*, Hunan Province)

Mount Heng, also known as Mount Xunlou (*Xunlou Shan*) or Mount Tiger (*Hu Shan*), is one of the five sacred mountains in China. It is located in the Nanyue District of Hengyang City, Hunan Province close to the Xiangjiang River at 1,300 meters above sea level. It has a reputation as "the Superior of the Five Sacred Mountains". Mount Heng is a granite fault-block mountain range across eight cities and counties in Hunan Province with Returning Geese Peak (*Huiyan Feng*) of Hengyang to the south and Mount Yuelu of Changsha to the north. The mountain range is 50 kilometers long and 20 kilometers wide consisting of 72 mountain peaks known as "seventy-two hibiscus in the sky", of which the five highest are *Zhurong*

南岳大庙 (图片提供：FOTOE)
South Sacred Mountain Temple

南起衡阳回雁峰，北至长沙岳麓山，横跨湖南省8个市县，长约50公里，宽20公里，由72座各具特色的山峰组成，亦被称作"青天七十二芙蓉"，其中祝融、紫盖、天柱、付融、石廪五峰最高。优越的地理环境带给衡山灵动娟秀的人间胜景：祝融峰高耸入云，水帘洞如梦如幻，藏经殿庄严灵秀，方广寺幽静深远。衡山的秀美吸引着历代名

Peak, Purple Chariot Cover Peak (*Zigai Feng*), Heavenly Pillar Peak (*Tianzhu Feng*), *Furong* Peak, and Stone Warehouse Peak (*Shilin Feng*). The advantages of Mount Heng's location and environment provide gorgeous mountain scenery such as the soaring *Zhurong* Peak, dreamlike Water Curtain Cave (*Shuilian Dong*), the dignified Sutras Hall (*Cangjing Dian*), and the serene Mahayana Sutras Temple (*Fangguang Si*). Its scenic beauty attracted noted literary figures of different dynasties to appreciate flowers in the spring, clouds in the summer, sun shinning in the fall and snow in the winter leaving behind many poems and verses.

Mount Heng is also a center of religion and culture in South China. Over thousands of years, Buddhism, Taoism and Confucianism integrated each other and blossomed in the beautiful mountainscape of Mount Heng. Along the mountain passageways or on the top of precipitous peaks or amidst lush green vegetation are dotted with historical sites such as the South Sacred Mountain Temple (*Nanyue Damlao*), Magic Mirror Terrace (*Mojing Tai*), South Terrace Temple (*Nantai Si*), Sutras Hall (*Cangjing Dian*), Mahayana Sutras Temple (*Fangguang Si*) and South Sacred

人雅士春观花、夏看云、秋望日、冬赏雪，留下了许多诗词。

同时，衡山也是南中国的宗教文化中心。千百年来，佛、道、儒互相渗透融合，在衡山这块灵秀的土地上绽放出朵朵智慧之花。沿着山间小径，或在陡峭的峰峦之巅，或在葱郁的林木之间，南岳大庙、磨镜台、南台寺、藏经殿、方广寺、南岳书院等名胜古迹隐藏其间，地理与人文、山水和文化和谐统一、水乳交融。

南岳大庙

衡山脚下的南岳大庙是一组集民间祠庙、佛教寺院、道教宫观和皇宫殿宇于一体的古建筑群，也是中国南方及五岳之中规模最大的庙宇。南岳大庙始建于唐代初年，历经六次大火和十六次重修。它的中轴线上呈现的是儒家建筑风格，东边为八座道观，西边为八座佛寺。正殿圣帝殿规模宏大，建筑巍峨，占地面积达1877平方米，是南岳大庙乃至南岳古镇上最高的建筑。整个殿宇结构精密复杂，雕梁画栋，凸显出崇高的地位。殿内供奉着

Mountain Academy (*Nanyue Shuyuan*). Mount Heng demonstrates a perfect integration and harmony between human geography and mountainscape culture.

South Sacred Mountain Temple (*Nanyue Damiao*)

At the foot of Mount Heng stands the South Sacred Mountain Temple, which is a group of ancient building structures that bring folk temples, Buddhist and Taoist monasteries and imperial palace halls into one grand complex. It is the largest temple both in the five sacred mountains and in South China. Constructed in the early Tang Dynasty, it went through 6 fires and 16 rebuilds. Built along the central axis are structures of Confucius architectural style including eight Taoist temples on the east side and eight Buddhist temples on the west side. The main Majestic Emperor Hall (Shengdi Dian) is a towering building of large scale covering a total of 1,877 square meters. It is the highest building in the South Sacred Mountain temple complex and even the Nanyue Old Town. The entire temple has very sophisticated layout with richly ornamented carved beams to highlight its lofty image. Inside the complex enshrines the statue of the South Sacred

"南岳司天昭圣帝"祝融，四周立有72根石柱，代表着衡山的72座山峰。殿堂内外到处可见神态各异、活灵活现的蛟龙，更有144块双面汉白玉浮雕生动演绎着《山海经》中的典故，不仅在建筑层面，在艺术层面也堪称一绝！这座古老的殿宇在苍天古木的掩映下，在静静流淌的历史长河中历久弥新，香火鼎盛，至今仍吸引着无数的信徒、游客前往朝拜、参观。

Mountain God of Zhurong surrounded by 72 stone pillars representing the 72 peaks of Mount Heng. Carved fluttering dragons can be seen everywhere inside and outside the temple. Stories in the *Classic of Mountains and Seas* (*Shanhai Jing*) are vividly depicted on 144 double-sided white marble reliefs demonstrating superb artistic and architectural work. Nestled under the towering old trees, this ancient temple has revived its life and attracted numerous pilgrims and tourists to come and visit.

《山海经》

《山海经》是一部富于神话传说的最古老的地理奇书，主要记述了中国古代的地理、物产、神话、巫术、宗教等，也包括古史、医药、民俗、民族等方面的内容。全书现存18卷，约3万字。《山海经》不仅具有文学价值和地理价值，它还是一部科技史，既记载了古代科学家们的创造发明，也有他们的科学实践活动，反映了当时的科学思想以及已经达到的科学技术水平。

Classic of Mountains and Seas (Shanhai Jin)

Classic of Mountains and Seas is the oldest fabled geographical and cultural of ancient China. The content includes geography, natural resources, mythology, witchcraft, religion, ancient history, medicine, folk customs and ethnicity, etc. There are 18 chapters of about 30,000 Chinese characters. *Classic of Mountains and Seas* not only has value in literature and geography, but also the history of technology documented ancient scientific and technological inventions and experiments by ancient scientists. This book reflects the scientific thinking and the scientific and technological level achieved at the time.

祝融

相传祝融氏是上古轩辕黄帝的一位大臣,当时的百姓虽然发明了钻木取火,但却不会保存火种,而且不会用火。黄帝于是任命祝融氏为管火的官员,将用火的方法传授给百姓。祝融死后,葬在南岳衡山,后人为了纪念他,就把南岳最高峰称为祝融峰。相传祝融喜爱音乐,他在衡山居住时,常常在山上奏起悠扬动听的乐曲,让百姓们精神振奋,更加热爱生活。

Zhu Rong

According to legend, Zhu Rong was a minister of the Emperor Huang. At that time, even though the technique to rub sticks to get fire was already invented, people did not know how to keep the fire for ignition and how to use fire. The Emperor Huang appointed Zhu Rong as the official to manage fire and teach people how to use fire. When he died, Zhu Rong was buried in Mount Heng. In memory of Zhu Rong, the highest peak of Mount Heng was named after him. It is said that he also loved music. When he lived in Mount Heng, people always heard his melodies, which made them happy and love their life more.

水帘洞

水帘洞位于衡山紫盖峰下,夹于吐雾、香炉两峰之间,人称"紫盖仙洞"。水帘洞古名"朱陵洞""仙人池",相传是梁朝的九位真人白日飞升的栖息之地,后建造九仙观以纪念他们。水帘洞附近水源丰富,泉水众多,太阳泉、洗心泉、洞真源、仙人池等都汇聚于此。汩汩溪水自四面八方汇聚于水帘洞上方的谷底,然后从石壁上飞

Water Curtain Cave (*Shuilian Dong*)

The Water Curtain Cave (*Shuilian Dong*) is at the foot of the Purple Chariot Cover Peak (*Zigai Feng*) of Mount Heng between the Misty Fog Peak (*Tuwu Feng*) and the Incense Burner Peak (*Xianglu Feng*). People call it "Purple Chariot Cover Celestial Cave" (*Zigai Xiandong*). Its ancient names were "Red Ridge Cave" (*Zhuling Dong*) and "Celestial Pool" (*Xianren Chi*). It is said that this was the rest place of the nine immortals

衡山水帘洞 (图片提供: FOTOE)
Water Curtain Cave in Mount Heng

流直泻而下，形成了20余丈的瀑布。瀑布水流湍急，飞珠溅玉，声如巨浪，气势逼人，如同一幅生动而壮观的珠帘挂在山腰。

方广寺

方广寺位于莲花峰石梁飞瀑旁，相传为五百罗汉栖息之处。方广寺始建于梁武帝天监二年（503年），南岳高僧慧海曾在这里诵经修行。方广寺在谷中分上、中、下三寺，历经毁建，现在尚存方广寺，内有山门、大雄宝殿、五百罗汉殿、会佛堂、地藏殿、伫真堂、

in the Liang Dynasty before they flew to heaven. Later the Nine Immortals Temple was built here to commemorate them. Rich in water resources, the Water Curtain Cave is surrounded by Sun Spring (*Taiyang Quan*), Clearing Evil Thoughts Spring (*Xixin Quan*), Immortal Cave Water (*Dongzhen Yuan*) and Immortals Pool (*Xianren Chi*). When streams from all directions flow into the bottom of the valley at the top of the Water Curtain Cave, the water rushes straight down from the cliff forming a waterfall of over 33 meters high with splashing water drops, roaring sound and intimidating water flow. It looks like a spectacular curtain made of pearls hanging over the mountainside.

Mahayana Sutras Temple (*Fangguang Si*)

Located next to the Stone Beam Waterfall (*Shiliang Feipu*) in Lotus Peak (*Lianhua Feng*), the Mahayana Sutras Temple (*Fangguang Si*) is said to be the residence of five hundred Arhats. Built in the year of 503 during the Liang Dynasty, the eminent monk Huihai of the South Sacred Mountain once lived in this temple chanting and practicing scriptures. The complex used to have three courtyards

衡山梵音谷 (图片提供: FOTOE)
梵音谷树林奇茂，溪水被大坝截流，景色十分幽美。
Valley of Buddha Sound (*Fanyin Gu*)
The Valley of Buddha Sound has beautiful scenery of lush green vegetation and streams blocked by a big dam.

左右厢房等建筑。五百罗汉堂内供奉五百罗汉塑像，神态各异，栩栩如生。整座建筑群隐秘在幽深的溪谷之中，在寺中可听到石涧潭瀑布的清脆击水声，抬头可看到竹树秀蔚，林荫蔽日，古有"不至方广，不足以知其深"之说。

built in the upper, middle and lower part of the valley. Destroyed several times and the lower part is the only one that survived. Inside there are the front gate, the Mahavira Hall, the Five Hundred Arhats Hall, the Meeting Buddha Hall, Ksitigarbha Hall, *Zhuzhen* Hall as well as supplementary rooms on the left and right wings. The Arhats Hall enshrines five hundred life-like Arhats with different looks and manners. All the structures were hidden deep in the valley with clear splashing water heard in the temple covered by gorgeous green bamboos and shady woods. There is an ancient saying "never know how deep the temple is until you come in."

> 西岳华山

华山位于陕西省华阴市境内，距古城西安100公里，北临黄河，南靠秦岭，西望长安。华山由一块巨大完整的花岗岩构成，"削成而四方，其广十里，高五千仞"，整个山体线条简洁，形如刀削斧劈，奇峰突兀，巍峨壮丽。华山共有东、西、南、北、中五座主峰，其中南峰"落雁"、东峰"朝阳"、西峰"莲花"三峰鼎峙耸立，有"天外三峰"之称。华山以"险"著称，被誉为"天下奇险第一山"。华山上山道路仅有北坡南北一线，约10公里长，沿着溪谷逶迤曲折，艰险崎岖，颇有"一夫当关，万夫莫开"的气概。悬崖峭壁上各种建筑依山而建，南峰山腰上凌空架设的长空栈道，峭壁绝崖上凿出的千尺

> West Sacred Mountain: Mount Hua (*Hua Shan*)

Mount Hua, situated in Huayin City, Shaanxi Province, is about 100 kilometers east of the ancient city Xi'an neighboring the Yellow River to the north, Mount Qin to the south and Xi'an to the west. Made up of a mountain of granite domes, Mount Hua is described as "whittled into a perfect square as wide as ten miles and as deep as five thousand *Ren* (ancient Chinese measuring unit)". The mountain silhouette is simple and clear-cut as if it was sculpted by a knife or chopped by an ax. Five main towering peaks abruptly stand out in the east, west, south, north and center of the mountain. The three highest peaks known as "three peaks in the outer sky" are the South Peak "Landing Goose" (*Luoyan Feng*), the East Peak "Sunrise" (*Chaoyan Feng*) and the West Peak "Lotus" (*Lianhua Feng*).

幢、百尺峡以及三面临空的鹞子翻身等都是华山险道中的险中之险。

华山除了壮丽的自然景观外，同时又有丰富的历史文化积淀，人文景观比比皆是。历代帝王黄帝、尧、舜、秦始皇、汉武帝、武则天、唐明皇等，都曾到华山进行过大规模的祭祀活动。李白、杜甫等文人墨客也曾多次攀登华山，留下

Mount Hua is renowned for its steepness and acclaimed as the "No. 1 Outrageously Precipitous Mountain". There is only one ascending route about 10 kilometers long from south to north in the northern side of the mountain. The narrow twisting pathway winds up around the ridges and gorges giving the impression described as "one man can hold out against ten thousand". Various structures were built

• 华山风光
Scenery of Mount Hua

• 华山日月岩

日月岩位于华山天梯之上，因岩上有两个圆形石纹，与日月相似而得名。

Sun and Moon Rock in Mount Hua

The Sun and Moon Rock is at the end of the Celestial Stairway (*Tianti*) in Mount Hua. The name came from two round stone marks on the rock resembling the sun and the moon.

诸多佳话。登临华山，仅山上山下及峪道沿途的题字、诗文、石刻就会使人流连忘返。华山还是道教圣地，被称为"第四洞天"，很多著名的道教高人都在此修行过。山上现存72个半悬空洞，道观20余座，其中玉泉院、东道院、镇岳宫被列为中国重点道教宫观。

along the contours of the mountain. The most dangerous places include a plank path built along the surface of a vertical cliff (*Changkong Zhandao*) at the South Peak, the Thousand Feet Pillar Path (*Qianchi Zhuang*) and the Hundred Feet Valley Path (*Baichi Xia*), both being chiseled on extremely steep cliffs as well as Hawk Overturn Path (*Yaozi Fanshen*) with only one side chained on a perpendicular cliff.

In addition's to its magnificent scenery, historical and cultural landscapes can be seen everywhere in Mount Hua. Emperors of different dynasties including the Emperor Huang, Emperor Yao, Emperor Shun, First Emperor of the Qing Dynasty, Emperor Wu of the Han Dynasty, Empress Wu Zetian and Emperor Xuanzong of the Tang Dynasty all held large-scale ritual ceremonies in Mount Hua. Famous poets such as Li Bai and Du Fu climbed Mount Hua several times leaving many much-told stories. It is hard for visitors to forget rock inscriptions, autographs, poems and verses carved on stones along the pathways up and down in the mountain. Mount Hua is also one of the Taoist sacred sites known as "the 4th Celestial Cavern" as many eminent monks

华山险道

千尺幢位于玉泉院与北峰之间，是登上华山的第一道险关。千尺幢开发始于汉代，是在峭壁最陡峭的地方开凿出一条一人宽的山路，凿刻出石梯370余阶，并在旁边安装粗大牢固的锁链供人攀爬。整个道路形如崖壁之间形成的天然缝隙，四周的峭壁刀削斧凿、高耸入云，唯有脚下仅能容下三分之一脚掌的石梯一阶一阶延伸至头顶处的一线天光，如同通天之梯一般；回望来路，只见道路深不可测，如临深渊。人们走在这条路上可谓惊心动魄，必须手脚并用、奋力攀爬。千尺幢的顶端有一个仅容一人的石洞，叫作"天井"。"天井"上有一平台，由于地势险峻，一人当关万人莫开，因此被形象地称为"太华咽喉"。

登上千尺幢，还有一条46米长几乎呈90°的险道——百尺峡。百尺峡又名"百丈崖"，是与千尺幢齐名的著名险道。百尺峡开凿于明末清初，共有91级台阶凌空一般开凿在一块倚悬崖缝隙而立的巨石之上。百尺峡虽然仅有46米，却势

practice Taoism here. Still existing today in Mount Hua are seventy-two half-suspended caves on cliff sides and twenty-two Taoist temples including the Jade Spring Temple (*Yuquan Yuan*), East Taoist Cloister (*Dongdao Yuan*) and Securing Mountain Palace (*Zhenyue Gong*) which are all officially listed as the key Taoist temples in China.

Dangerous Pathways in Mount Hua

The No. 1 precipitous pathway to ascend Mount Hua is the Thousand Feet Pillar Path (*Qianchi Zhuang*) between the Jade Spring Cloister and the North Peak. During the Han Dynasty (206 B.C.- 220 A.D.), a narrow pathway of a person's body width was built in the steepest cliff area with over 370 chiseled stone steps. Big thick chains were installed securely to assist climbers. The pathway looks like a natural rock crevice surrounded by sheer cliffs soaring to the sky. Each step is only one third of a person's foot. Using both hands and feet with all efforts, it is thrilling and frightening to climb up one step at a time towards a thin strip of skylight at the top as if one walked up a ladder to heaven when looking back the pathway seemed to fall into an abyss.

危坡陡，直插云表，而且头顶上有"惊心石"，摇摇欲坠，其险比千尺幢有过之而无不及。

At the very top of the pathway there is a cave can only accommodate one person. The cave is called the "Celestial Well" (*Tianjing*) and has a stage. It is vividly described as the "throat of imperial Hua" because of its precipitous position and its reputation of "one man can hold out against ten thousand"

Equally famous for its precipitousness is another 46-meter long perpendicular path called the Hundred Feet Valley Path (*Baichi Xia*), also known as Hundred Yard Cliff (*Baizhang Ya*). It was first constructed during late Ming Dynasty and early Qing Dynasty. Ninety-one stone steps were chiseled on a huge rock inserted in a cliff crevice as if they were hanging from the sky. Even though it is only 46 meters long, with a nerve-racking shaky rock over the head, this extremely steep pathway is no better than the Thousand Feet Pillar path.

● 华山险道
华山自古以来就是探险爱好者的天地，有"走路不看景，看景不走路"之说。

Precipitous Pathways in Mount Hua
Since ancient times Mount Hua has always been a paradise for adventure lovers. There is a saying among Mount Hua hikers, "no scenery viewing while walking and no walking while viewing the scenery".

华山松

华山松又名"五针松",高大挺拔,树皮呈灰绿色,叶为五针一束,冠形优美、姿态奇特,是华山的一大奇景。不仅如此,华山松那傲然屹立的姿态和傲霜斗雪的品格,能传递奋发向上的精神,因而被世人视为楷模,在民间被视为延年益寿、长青不老的象征。华山松喜在温凉湿润的气候中生长,不耐寒及湿热,因此集中生长在华山一带。

Pine Trees in Mount Hua

Pine trees in Mount Hua also known as "five-needle pines" are upright and tall with a grayish green color and leaves in fascicles of five needles. Growing in elegant and unique shapes, they are considered one of the wonders of Mount Hua. They are respected by people because they represent a hardworking and upward spirit of standing up proudly and fighting against fog and snow. They are also a symbol of longevity and forever youth among people. These pine trees concentrate in Mount Hua because they prefer the well-drained soil and cool humid climate.

- 华山松
  Pine Trees in Mount Hua

玉泉院

　　玉泉院位于华山脚下，是华山道教活动的主要场所。玉泉院中有一弯泉水。相传在唐朝的时候，金仙公主在山上镇岳宫的玉井中汲水洗头，不慎将玉簪掉入水中，后来却在玉泉院院中的泉水中找了回来，方知此泉与玉井相通，于是赐名此泉为"玉泉"，玉泉院也因此得名。玉泉院为江南园林建筑风格，是道士贾得升为师傅陈抟

Jade Spring Temple (*Yuquan Yuan*)

Located at the foot of Mount Hua, Jade Spring Temple is one of the main Taoist temples in China. There is a spring pond in the center. It is said that Princess Golden Fairy of the Tang Dynasty lost her jade hairpin in the Jade Well in the Secure Mountain Palace (*Zhenyue Gong*). Later the hairpin was found in the spring water pond in Jade Spring Temple, which made people realize that the jade well and the spring pond were connected. Therefore the spring pond changed its name as Jade

- 华山大朝元洞

大朝元洞是元代初年道士贺志真修身养性之所，沿华山峪谷选址凿建。

Dachaoyuan Cavern in Mount Hua

Cavern was the self-cultivation place built for Taoist priest He Zhizhen of early Yuan Dynasty. He personal selected this place in a Mount Hua valley.

劈山救母

传说汉代的刘向与仙女三圣母有三世姻缘，最终在华山神庙与三圣母相遇，并结为夫妻。在离别的时候，刘向赠与三圣母一块沉香，告诉她若日后有子，以此为名。后来，三圣母果真有孕，这件事被她的哥哥二郎神知道了，一怒之下将她囚禁于华山的某个洞穴中。三圣母在洞中产下一子，命名"沉香"，并托人将其送与刘向。沉香长大后来到华山寻母，在仙姑的帮助下学习仙法，偷得神斧，劈山救母。现在，华山西峰顶上，尚有一块截为三节的巨石，巨石旁插着一把月牙铁斧。

The Story of Breaking up the Mountain to Save Mother

According to legend, a scholar named Liu Xiang in the Han Dynasty had a relationship with San Shengmu for three generations. They eventually met in a celestial temple in Mount Hua and got married. Upon leaving, Liu Xiang gave San Shengmu an aquilaria (*Chenxiang*) as a gift and asked her to name their baby after the gift. Later when she really got pregnant, her brother God Erlang heard about it and furiously locked her up in a cave in Mount Hua. She gave birth to a boy in the cave and named him Chenxiang, who was later sent to his father. When he grew up, Chenxiang came to Mount Hua looking for his mother. With the help of a fairy, he mastered some magic skills. He stole a magic ax and broke up the mountain to get his mother out. Today at the West Peak of Mount Hua, there is a huge rock broken up in three sections beside which an iron ax of crescent moon shape was fixed on the ground.

• 华山风光
Scenery of Mount Hua

老祖于宋仁宗皇祐年间修建的。玉泉院的主体建筑大殿分前殿和后殿，前殿是道士们举行各种活动的地方，供奉着道教华山派的创始人——郝大通，后殿供奉陈抟的坐像。玉泉院环境优美，布局严密，园中泉水汩汩，古木苍苍，七十二窗长廊风格独特、形态各异，亭榭殿阁布局巧妙、相映成趣，更有无数名人碑刻，熠熠生辉。

Spring, so as the the Jade Spring Temple. It was constructed between 1049 and 1051 of the Song Dynasty dedicating to Jia De, a legendary Taoist sage. Built in the architectural style of classical gardens in south China, the main complex is divided into two halls, the front hall and the back hall. The front hall has a shrine for Hao Datong, the founder of Mount Hua Taoist sec and is used by Taoist monks to perform various functions. The back hall has a shrine for Jia De. In a well-organized layout and enchanting environment, the temple is embellished by quietly flowing spring water, tall ancient pine trees, a unique long corridor of seventy-two windows, pavilions and terraces as well as numerous stone inscriptions of noted scholars.

咏华山（宋 寇准）

只有天在上，更无山与齐。
举头红日近，俯首白云低。

诗词译文：

头上只有高高的天空，四周没有哪座山峰能与它看齐。
抬头感觉太阳是那么的近，低头看见的是白云在低处飘荡。

Ode on Mount Hua by Kou Zhun, Song Dynasty (960-1297)

Poem Interpretation

Above high in the sky, no mountain peaks around comparable to Mount Hua;

Looking up at the red sun in close distance; when turning around you see white clouds floating below.

• 《华山胜景》（现代 张大千）
Scenic Beauty of Mount Hua by Zhang Daqian, Modern

> 北岳恒山

恒山，亦名"太恒山""元岳""紫岳""大茂山"，是五岳中的北岳。恒山位于山西省北部和河北省西北部，绵延150余公里，海拔2017米，山体横卧塞上，巍峨耸峙，延绵不绝，被称为"绝塞名山"。恒山号称"一百零八峰"，主峰天峰岭海拔2017米，被称为"人天北柱"。天峰岭山势雄伟，风景如画，与另一座主峰翠屏峰东西相望，如同双塔。两峰之间的金龙峡，峡谷幽深，峭壁侧立，青天一线，最窄处不足10米，形成绝塞天险。徐霞客在游记中生动描绘了这双峰的险峻："伊阙（河南龙门山）双峙、武夷九曲，俱不足以拟也。"

天然的地势使得这里成为护卫北京和黄河以北中原地区的天然屏

> North Sacred Mountain: Mount Heng (*Heng Shan*, Shanxi)

Mount Heng (*Heng Shan*), also named as "*Taiheng Shan*", "*Yuanyue*", "*Ziyue*" and "*Damao Shan*" is the north mountain of the five sacred mountains in China. Situated in north of Shanxi Province and northwest of Hebei Province, the mountain range stretches over 150 kilometers at an altitude of 2,017 meters. The magnificent Mount Heng extends continuously across the ancient northern frontier, lauded as "the best frontier mountain". Claimed to have one hundred and eight peaks, the main peak Heavenly Peak Ridge (*Tianfeng Ling*) is 2,017 meters above sea level known as the "Northern Pole between Heaven and Earth". The magnificent and picturesque Heavenly Peak Ridge stands opposite

● 恒山风光
Scenery of Mount Heng

障，又是通往蒙古高原的要塞，因此自古就是兵家必争之地。山上崖高谷深，山路崎岖，处处是苍松翠柏、鸟语花香，庙观楼阁、怪石幽洞星罗棋布，为恒山添抹上绝妙的妆容。

历史上，道教、佛教皆在此建立庙宇亭阁，讲经布道，曾有"一里一亭，一步一松，三寺四祠七亭阁，九宫八洞十五庙"之说。现在，恒山依然保存着规模宏大的古

the Green Screen Peak (*Cuiping Feng*) resembling twin towers. In between lies the deep and quite Golden Dragon Gorge (*Jinlong Xia*) surrounded by sheer cliffs with the narrowest place no more than 10 meters wide forming a natural barrier. Xu Xiake commented on the two precipitous peaks in his travel notes that "the twin peaks in *Yique* (Mount Longmen of Henan Province) and nine twisting streams of Mount Wuyi have no comparisons."

The natural terrain made this mountain

建筑群和众多珍贵文物，现存文物古迹及祭祀庙宇20多座（群）。翠屏、恒麓等书院学舍，摩崖石刻和各种楹联碑碣等，更为其增添了独特的魅力。

悬空寺

悬空寺位于恒山脚下的金龙峡内西岩峭壁上，是中国佛、道、儒合一的寺庙，号称"恒山第一胜

• 恒山悬空寺
Suspended Temple in Mount Heng

range a natural barrier for Beijing and the central plains north of the Yellow River and also the fortress leading to the Mongolian plateau. It had always been a military battleground in ancient times. Mount Heng's scenery is decorated with towering mountain summits, deep gorges, rugged trails, lush green vegetation, a variety of species, temples, pagodas and strangely shaped rocks and caves.

In history both Taoist and Buddhist temples were built in Mount Heng for teaching their own religion. There once was a saying, "a pavilion in every mile, a pine in every step, three monasteries, four ancestral halls, seven pavilions, nine palaces, eight caves and fifteen temples." Today Mount Heng still preserves large-scaled ancient building structures and many precious cultural relics including over 20 existing heritage sites and temples for sacrifice rituals, the Green Screen Academy (*Cuiping Shuyuan*), *Henglu* Academy, cliff-side carvings, stone couplets and steles, all of which have added a unique charm to Mount Heng.

Suspended Temple (*Xuankong Si*)

The Suspended Temple is located at the foot of Mount Heng clinging to the western part of cliff side in the Golden Dragon

景"，美国《时代》周刊将其列为全球十大最奇险建筑之一。悬空寺创建于北魏后期，拥有1500多年的历史。现存建筑是明、清两代修建后的遗物。恒山金龙峡山势陡峻，两边是斧劈刀削一般的悬崖，悬空寺背西面东建在悬崖上，背倚峭壁，面临深渊，凌空而置。寺内有两座三层木质建筑，中间以木桥连接，共计房间40间。殿内供奉佛、

- 恒山悬空寺
  Suspended Temple in Mount Heng

Gorge (*Jinlong Xia*). It is the temple in China that unified Buddhism, Taoism and Confucianism into one place known as the "No. 1 Scenic Wonder in Mount Heng". The TIME Magazine lists it as one of the top 10 precarious buildings in the world. The temple was built in the Northern Wei Dynasty over 1,500 years ago. The extant structures were restored in the Ming and Qing dynasties. The temple suspends over the mountain side facing the east with its back against sheer cliffs and its front confronting the deep abyss. Inside the temple there are two three-story wooden structures connected by wooden bridges with a total of 40 rooms. Buddhist, Taoist and Confucian ancestors are enshrined inside with a variety of exquisitely painted sculptures.

道、儒三家始祖，各种彩塑数目众多，造型精巧，徐霞客称其为"天下巨观"。

恒山悬空寺上戴危崖，下临深谷，楼阁悬空，远远望去异常惊险，好像一阵风吹过来就会倒下来似的。悬空寺的楼阁和栈道下埋有横梁，将整座寺庙牢牢地托起。这些横梁直径约50厘米，插在山岩中，就像是从岩石中长出来的。露在外面的横梁只是其中一小部分，大约有一米长，而插进山岩的部分据推测要长得多。

Xu Xiake called it "the greatest wonder in the world".

It is exceptionally breathtaking to see the Suspended Temple clinging to the cliff in mid-air with a deep valley below as if a gust of wind could send the structures tumbling off the cliff. Its buildings and plank pathways are securely kept in place with wooden crossbeams of 50 centimeters in diameter chiseled into the rocks as if they grew out of the cleft. Only a small section of the crossbeam, about one meter long, extends out from the cliff. The section that was chiseled into the rocks is estimated to be a lot longer.

千年不腐的恒山悬空寺

作为木制寺庙群，恒山悬空寺经历了1500多年来的山崩、地震和雨水的侵蚀，始终屹立不倒。木头是很容易腐烂的，而悬空寺的横梁虽然有些已经开裂，但却没有腐烂，这是为什么呢？原来，这些横梁都是由铁杉木制成的。铁杉木质地十分细密，耐磨性很好，不易变形和开裂。而且，横梁全部用桐油泡过，具有抗病虫、耐酸、耐碱和防腐的作用。另外，悬空寺所处的翠屏峰呈一个内收的弧形，对面山峰也呈一个内收的弧形，两座山峰就好像两只手一样包拢着悬空寺，使得全寺很难被阳光直射，避免了暴晒。

Undecayed Suspended Temple of Mount Heng

The wooden structures of the Suspended Temple experienced over 1,500 years of landslides, earthquakes and rain erosion, but they still remain standing. Usually it is very easy for wood to get rotten. The crossbeams used in this temple never rotted even though there are cracks in some places. Why is this? It turns out that they were made of hemlock, which has fine quality and very durable, hard to get deformation or cracks. In addition all the crossbeams were soaked in tung oil to be resist insects, acid, alkali and corrosion. The peaks on both sides of the temple have a concave resembling two hand palms enclosing the structures. The concave shape makes it hard for the sun to shine through, thus preventing the structures' exposure to the sunlight.

• 恒山悬空寺的内部构造
Inner Structure of the Suspended Temple in Mount Heng

北岳庙

北岳庙又称"恒宗殿""贞元殿"等，俗称"朝殿"，位于天峰岭南面的石壁之下，始建于

North Mountain Temple (*Beiyue Miao*)

The North Mountain Temple (*Beiyue Miao*), also called *Hengzong* Hall, *Zhenyuan* Hall, or commonly known as *Chao Dian*, is situated to the south of the

● 北岳庙 (图片提供: FOTOE)
North Mountain Temple

明代弘治年间，是恒山最为宏伟的一座庙。经过五百多年的毁建，北岳庙现存古建筑主要有御香亭、凌霄门、山门、飞石殿遗址和德宁之殿等。北岳庙正殿四周有回廊环绕，殿内供奉着头戴天平冠，身披朱绫袍的北岳大帝塑像。神座上方高悬清代康熙皇帝御书匾额"化垂悠久"，两旁恭立四位文官和四大元帅像。北岳庙碑碣林立，现存北魏、北齐、唐、宋、元、明、清各代碑碣137通，各种书体都具备，在

Heavenly Peak Ridge (*Tianfeng Ling*) below the cliffs. Built in 1501 during the Ming Dynasty, it is the most majestic among all Mount Heng's temples. After hundreds of years of destructions and rebuilds, the extant ancient structures include the Imperial Fragrance Pavilion (*Yuxiang Ting*), Soaring Gate (*Lingxiao Men*), the front gate (*Shanmen*), Flying Stone Hall (*Feishi Dian*) remnants and Dening Hall (*Dening Dian*). The main hall of the North Mountain Temple is surrounded by corridors. Inside a shrine is dedicated to the Great North Sacred

一定程度上代表了不同时期的书法艺术水平，具有很高的艺术价值，为中国现存的书法艺术珍品。

飞石窟

飞石窟位于恒山飞石峰山腰，是一个三面环壁，一面临崖的天然大石窟。窟内面积大约200平方米，呈方形，建有北岳寝宫。北岳寝宫曾是北岳正殿，但随着恒山的扩建，另建恒宗殿为主殿，北岳寝宫便成了北岳大帝夫人的寝宫。关于飞石窟，还有一个美丽的传说。相传4000多年前，舜帝北巡，在祭

Mountain statue of the God of wearing the *Tianping* (literally balance) crown and a red silk robe. Above the shrine hangs a horizontal tablet inscribed "*Huachui Youjiu*", which means the merit of educating the people in the way of nature. It was awarded by Emperor Kangxi of the Qing Dynasty. Besides, portraits of four civilian officials and four military generals stand respectfully on each side. There are over 137 stone tablets from North Wei, North Qi, Tang, Song, Yuan, Ming and Qing dynasties in the temple inscribed with different calligraphical styles representing the artistic level of calligraphy in each period. They have high artistic value and they are treasures of Chinese calligraphic art.

• 恒山飞石窟
Flying Rock Cavern in Mount Heng

祀恒山的时候突然天降飞石，于是舜帝就把这块飞石命名为"安王石"。五年之后，舜帝再度北巡。由于时值寒冬腊月，大雪阻住了去恒山的道路，舜帝只得停在河北省曲阳县遥祭恒山。正当此时，那块飞石再次从天而降，从恒山飞到了曲阳。而它在恒山曾经待过的地方就出现了一个硕大、幽深的洞窟，被后人称为"飞石窟"。

应县木塔

恒山脚下有一座应县木塔，与巴黎埃菲尔铁塔和比萨斜塔并称为"世界三大奇塔"。木塔高67.31米，底层直径30.27米，呈平面八角形，外观五层，底层扩出一圈外廊，与底屋塔身的屋檐构成重檐，所以共有六重塔檐。每层下面都有一个暗层，因而结构实为九层。暗层的外观是平座，设有栏杆，可以凭栏远眺。塔内存有大量辽代典藏。近千年来，应县木塔除经受了四季变化、风霜雨雪的侵蚀外，还曾遭受过多次强地震的袭击，然而至今却依然屹立不倒。

应县木塔结构精巧，材料结实，

Flying Rock Cavern (*Feishi Ku*)

Flying Rock Cavern (*Feishi Ku*) at the half way up to the Mount Heng is a huge natural cavern with an internal square of 200 square meters surrounded by stone walls on three sides and the cliff on one side. Inside there is the North Mountain Hall (*Beiyue Dian*), which was once the main hall in the cavern. With the expansion of building structures in Mount Heng, *Hengzong* Hall was built and became the main hall. As a result the North Mountain Hall turned into a living quarter for the Goddess of North Mountain. There is also a beautiful legend about the Flying Rock Cavern. It is said that over 4,000 years ago on his cruise in North China, Emperor Shun saw a flying rock falling down from the sky and he named the rock "*Anwang* Rock". Five years later, he went on a cruise to the north again during a cold winter. When snow blocked the road to Mount Heng, the emperor had to stop at Quyang County of Hebei Province to pay homage to Mount Heng remotely. Right at this moment, the same flying rock came down from the sky again, flying from Mount Heng to Quyang County. And the place where the rock used to be turned into a huge deep cavern, hence the name "Flying Rock Cavern".

应县木塔
Wooden Pagoda in Ying County

应县木塔内景
Interior view of Wooden Pagoda in Ying County

Wooden Pagoda in Ying County (*Yingxian Muta*)

At the foot of Mount Heng stands the wooden pagoda of Ying County reaching a total height of 67.31 meter on a round platform of 30.27 meters in diameter. It is considered as one of the three wonderful towers in the world comparable to the Eiffel Tower in Paris and the Leaning Tower of Pisa. It has an appearance of an octagon with five stories and an extended terrace built at the bottom platform, which formed double eaves parallel to the pagoda roof. Therefore the pagoda has six doubled pagoda eaves. Under each story hides a mezzanine layer so that the interior of the pagoda actually reveals a nine-story structure between the roof and the bottom platform. The outer part of the hidden layer is built into a balcony for viewing. There are a large collection of cultural relic of the Liao Dynasty (907-1125). The pagoda has withstood seasonal changes and erosions from rain and snow. It also stood firm after many earthquakes.

The main reason why the pagoda never collapsed over a thousand years lies in its light structure, durable building materials and the unique local climate,

同时当地气候独特，易于木质材料保存，这些都是保证木塔千年不倒的主要原因。应县木塔采用的是分层叠合的明暗层结构，用体积很小的木料组成了庞大的塔身，现代许多高层建筑就是采用这种办法建造的。

which helps to retain the quality of the wood. The pagoda's architecture adopted layered composite design and a combination of visible and hidden structures using light and small wooden materials to build a huge pagoda body, which is a concept used by many high-rises today.

张果老的传说

恒山是道教的发祥地之一，传说八仙之一的张果老就曾在恒山隐居潜修，并在恒山留下了大量的仙踪遗迹和神话传说。据《唐书》记载，张果老确有其人，是广宗的一个道人。由于他名声鼎盛，曾经屡次得到过唐太宗、唐高宗、唐玄宗等皇帝的召见。唐玄宗誉其"迹先高尚，心入窅冥"，赐号"通玄先生"。相传，恒山的悬根松就是他坐骑白驴的"杰作"。有一天，张果老将白驴拴在一棵松树上。突然，从山里跑出一只白额吊睛猛虎。白驴为保性命，与这只猛虎殊死搏斗，在激烈的对抗中，硬生生将这棵拴着它的松树连根拔起，树干上也留下了明显的痕迹。张果老赶到后看到如此情景赶紧将树木扶正，并念咒修复。此后，这棵根系暴露在外的松树成了恒山一景。沿着悬根松北上的山路是一块光滑的陡石坡，有几个浅浅的石窝，酷似驴的蹄印，相传是张果老骑毛驴由此登天时留下的。

Legend about Zhang Guolao

Mount Heng is one of the birthplaces of Taoism. According to legend, Zhang Guolao, one of the eight Taoist immortals, once lived here as a hermit to practice Taoism, thus leaving behind many mythical stories and relics. *The Book of Tang* records that there was actually a Taoist priest from Guangzong (today's Guangzong County, Hebei Province) named Zhang Guolao during the Tang Dynasty (618-907). He was summoned several times by Emperor Taizong, Emperor Gaozong and Emperor Xuanzong of Tang Dynasty due to his popularity. Emperor Xuanzong even bestowed him the title "Master of Mysteries" praising his reasoning and lofty manners. It is said that the Pine of Suspended Root (*Xuangen Song*) on Mount Heng was his work while riding his white donkey. One day, Zhang Guolao tied his white donkey to a pine tree. Suddenly a tiger with a white forehead and slanted eye tiger jumped out. To protect its own life, the white donkey fought the tiger fiercely and uprooted the pine tree. Zhang Guolao set the tree straight again by chanting magic spells. With its roots visible above the ground, the pine tree became a scenic spot on Mount Heng. Along the Pine of Suspended Root to the north, there is a smooth steep rock with a few shallow marks resembling a donkey's footprints. It is said that those were left by the white donkey which Zhang Guolao rode it to heaven.

- 《八仙图》（清 黄慎）

  八仙是中国民间广为流传的道教八位神仙，分别为铁拐李、汉钟离、张果老、蓝采和、何仙姑、吕洞宾、韩湘子和曹国舅，其中以张果老（图右一）岁数最人。

  Painting of Eight Immortals by Huang Shen of Qing Dynasty (1616-1911)

  The eight immortals are eight deities in the Chinese folklore. They are Tieguai Li, Han Zhongli, Zhang Guolao, Lan Caihe, He Xiangu, Lv Dongbin, Han Xiangzi and Cao Guojiu. Zhang Guolao is the oldest.

佛教名山
Famous Buddhist Mountains

    中国有四大佛教名山，即五台山、峨眉山、九华山、普陀山。这四大名山随着佛教的传入，从汉代开始建寺庙，修道场，一直延续至清末，具有深厚的佛教文化底蕴。

There are four famous Buddhist Mountains in China: Mount Wutai (*Wutai Shan*), Mount Emei (*Emei Shan*), Mount Jiuhua (*Jiuhua Shan*) and Mount Putuo (*Putuo Shan*). With the introduction of Buddhism in China, constructions of Buddhist temples and practicing sites continued from the Han Dynasty through the end of the Qing Dynasty. These mountains are embedded with a profound Buddhist culture.

> 五台山

五台山位于中国山西省东北部，地处黄土高原，最高海拔达3058米，总面积为2837平方公里，是华北平原最高的山峰，被称为"华北屋脊"。五台山由五座山峰环抱而成。这五峰"耸出，顶无林木，有如垒土之台"，后按方位分为东台望海峰、西台挂月峰、南台锦绣峰、北台叶斗峰和中台翠岩峰，故名"五台山"；又因"岁积坚冰，夏仍飞雪，曾无炎暑"，因此又有"清凉山"之称。五台山风光秀丽，景色宜人，郁郁的森林和潺潺的溪水赋予其山峦叠错、沟壑纵横的奇特地形，有着令人赞叹的灵气。

与五台山如画风光交错相映的，是繁华的殿宇楼台和厚重的佛

> Mount Wutai (*Wutai Shan*)

Located in the Loess Plateau, northeast of Shanxi Province, Mount Wutai covers an area of 2387 square kilometers at an elevation of 3,058 meters. It is the highest mountain in the North China Plain known as the "Roof of North China Plain". Mount Wutai is embraced by five treeless flat terraced peaks, which were described as resembling "terraces built with soil" in ancient times. Geographically within Mount Wutai, the Sea Viewing Peak (*Wanghai Feng*) is located on the east terrace, Hanging Moon Peak (*Guayue Feng*) on the west terrace, Splendor Peak (*Jinxiu Feng*) on the south terrace, Lush Leaves Peak (*Yedou Feng*) on the north terrace, and Green Rocks Peak (*Cuiyan Feng*) in the central terrace, hence the name Mount Wutai meaning Mount Five Terraces. It is also known as the Cool

• 五台山风光 (图片提供：全景正片)
Scenery of Mount Wutai

教文化。自东汉永平年间由印度高僧摄摩腾和竺法兰建造第一座佛寺灵鹫寺之后，又经北魏、北齐、隋、唐直至清末不断修建，在这一千多年间，五台山佛寺遍布，建筑辉煌壮丽，最多时曾达数百所，僧侣万余人，成为中国极具影响力的佛教圣地。目前，五台山现存寺庙共47处。显通寺、塔院寺、罗睺寺、万佛阁、菩萨顶等著名的建筑如同星斗般坐落在风景如画的山峦

Mountain for "it has accumulated ice all-year round, snows in the summer and never has hot summer" as described in the Song Dynasty's *Legends of Cool Mountains*. The beauty of rising and falling ridges, exotic rocks, crisscrossed gullies, flowing creeks and lush green forests all give Mount Wutai impressive scenery.

Intertwined with its scenic beauty are the extravagant temples, halls and pavilions immersed deeply in the Buddhist culture. Since the first Buddhist temple

之间。雄伟气派的建筑、精美辉煌的雕刻绘画、珍贵丰富的文物古迹，以及千百年来积淀的灿烂文化成为五台山不可或缺的组成部分，是中国古建筑、雕塑、绘画的艺术宝库。

Vulture (*Lingjiu*) Temple was built by two Indian senior monks Kasyapamatanga and Dharmaratna between the year of 58 and 75 during the Eastern Han Dynasty, several hundred temples sprouted up all over Mount Wutai in the period of over a thousand years during the North Wei, North Qi, Sui, Tang and Late Qing dynasties. These splendid and magnificent temples were once the residence for over 10,000 Buddhist monks making Mount Wutai one of the most influential Buddhist sacred sites in China. Today there are 47 existing Buddhist building structures including *Xiantong* Temple, *Tayuan* Temple, *Luohou* Temple, Ten Thousand Buddha Tower (*Wanfou Ge*) and Bodhisattva Summit Temple (*Pusa Ding*), which are like stars dotted in the enchanting landscape of mountain ridges and gorges. The magnificent buildings, the exquisite statues, paintings and other precious cultural relics inside are an indispensable part of the Chinese treasures of ancient architecture, sculpture and fine art.

龙泉寺观音殿

五台山上的龙泉寺是非常著名的一座寺庙，相传是宋代杨家将的家庙。

Hall of Bodhisattva Guanyin (*Guanyin Dian*) in Dragon Spring Temple (*Longquan Si*)

The Dragon Spring Temple is a very famous temple in Mount Wutai. According to legend, it is the ancestral temple of General Yang's of the Song Dynasty.

台怀镇

台怀镇位于五大高峰的合拥环抱之中，是一个环山绕水风景秀丽的山镇。台怀镇上古建筑繁多，古刹寺院、楼台殿阁、宝塔牌坊四处可见，是五台山佛事活动和经济生活的中心。其中，镇上最引人注目的建筑是位于塔院寺的一座藏式大白塔，白塔

Taihuai Town

Taihuai Town is a small mountain town surrounded by the five towering peaks and the beautiful scenery. Ancient building structures such as temples, pagodas, pavilions and memorial gateways can be seen everywhere. It is the center of economic life and Buddhist activities in Mount Wutai. The most

- 台怀镇
  Taiwai Town

- 五台山塔院寺大白塔

大白塔全称"释迦牟尼舍利塔",塔身拔地而起凌空高耸,在五台山群寺的簇拥之下蔚为壮观。

Big White Dagoba in *Tayuan* Temple, Mount Wutai

The full name of the Big White Dagoba is Dagoba of Sakyamuni Buddha. Surrounded by a crowd of temples in Mount Wutai, the towering and magnificent white dagoba stands out abruptly from the ground.

高70多米,通体雪白,状如藻瓶,上下悬挂252枚铜铃随着清风丁零作响。

菩萨顶

菩萨顶始建于北魏时期,后来经过清朝顺治年间的重修,规模宏大,建筑富丽堂皇,为五台山诸寺之首。一条108级的台阶如同天梯一

striking building in the town is the Tibetan style white dagoba in the center of the *Tayuan* Temple complex. Painted white all over, it is 70 meters high and shaped like an ancient Chinese vase with 252 wind-bells hanging from its eaves.

Bodhisattva Summit Temple

Bodhisattva Summit Temple was first constructed in the North Wei Dynasty (386-534). It was rebuilt and expanded in the year of 1638 to 1661 during the Qing Dynasty. This grand temple structure is considered the best of all temples in Mount Wutai. A walkway of 108 stone steps leads to the summit as if it was a ladder to heaven from the temples below.

Xiantong Temple

Xiantong Temple is in the northern part of the Taihuai Town, one of the five Zen sites in Mount Wutai and the 2nd Buddhist temple in China after the White Horse Temple (*Baima Si*). It became the largest temple complex in Mount Wutai through a series of constructions in the North Wei, Tang, Ming and Qing dynasties. Inside the complex, buildings are very well preserved with an orderly layout of halls and subsidiary

五台山菩萨顶
Bodhisattva Summit Temple of Mount Wutai

般将寺庙与山下相连。

显通寺

显通寺位于台怀镇北侧，是五台山五大禅处之一。它历史悠久，是继白马寺之后中国的第二座寺庙；后经北魏、唐、明、清的扩建，最终形成宏大的规模，是五台山规模最大的寺庙。寺内建筑保存完好，殿堂、厢房布局严整，中轴线分明。地处中轴线的七重殿辉煌壮丽，尤其是其中的铜殿由青铜铸

rooms along the central axis. The most magnificent and unique are the seven levels of halls on the axis, one of which was totally cast in bronze. Five bronze pagodas are placed according to the five directions in front of the bronze hall with a Bodhisattva's statue sitting in the center inside. Cast outside of the walls are pictorial patterns of flowers and plants, birds and animals. The extant structure is considered a world's treasure for its elegant style, ingenious structure and exquisite craftsmanship.

The brass bell hanging in the bell

造，别具一格。殿前按照方位放置五座铜塔，隔扇外铸有36幅花卉鸟兽图案。铜殿造型优美、结构巧妙、工艺绝佳，是难得的珍品。

寺前的钟楼上悬挂着一口长鸣钟，铸造于明朝天启年间，据说重

tower in front of the temple was cast between 1621 and 1627 during the Ming Dynasty weighing and it is said this bell weighs 4999.75 kilograms. Outside of the bell cast over ten thousand words of Buddhist inscriptions. When the bell

• 五台山显通寺的钟楼
Bell Tower of *Xiantong* Temple in Mount Wutai

9999.5斤。这口钟的外部，铸有楷书佛经一部，共一万余字。因为敲击时钟声绵长，传播深远，所以人们又把此钟称为"长鸣钟"，也称为"长命钟"。

rings, the toll can be heard very far away. Therefore, it is called the "Long Toll Bell" (*Changming Zhong*), also known as the "Longevity Bell" because in Chinese "long toll" and "longevity" have the same pronunciation.

五台山的由来

传说，远古时代的五台山称为"五峰山"。那里气候异常恶劣，常年酷暑，当地百姓苦不堪言，时逢文殊菩萨在那里讲经说法，见到黎民百姓的疾苦，深表同情于是发大愿拯救百姓脱离苦海。文殊菩萨装扮成一个化缘的和尚，行程万里到东海龙王那里寻求帮助。他在龙宫门口发现了一块能散发凉风的巨大青石（东海龙王的歇龙宝石），于是便把它带了回来。当他把那块大青石放置在五峰山的一道山谷里时，那里一刹那间就变成了草丰水美、清凉无比的天然牧场。此后，那条山谷也被叫作"清凉谷"。人们在山谷里建了一座寺院，将那清凉石圈在院内。从此，五峰山又名"清凉山"。后来，隋文帝听说此传说后，便下诏在五座山峰的台顶各建一座寺院供奉文殊菩萨。即东台顶的聪明文殊，西台顶的狮子吼文殊，南台顶的智慧文殊，北台顶的无垢文殊，中台顶的孺童文殊。在东台顶能看日出，西台顶能赏明月，南台顶能观山花，北台顶能望瑞雪。这就是五台山的由来。

History of Mount Wutai

According to legend, Mount Wutai was called "Mount Five Peaks" (*Wufeng Shan*) in ancient times when the weather was unusually severe with intense summer heat all year round. When Manjusri Bodhisattva preached Buddhist teachings in that area, he felt very sympathetic about people's miserable sufferings. He dressed as a mendicant monk and traveled over 10 thousand miles to look for help from the Dragon King in the east sea. In front of the Dragon King's palace, he saw a big green stone that could generate a cool breeze and this stone turned out to be a precious stone of the Dragon King. He brought the stone back to Mount Wutai. As soon as it was placed in one of the valleys, the whole area turned into a cool natural pasture with green grass and clear water. Later people called the valley "cool valley" and built a temple to house the green and cool stone. From then on, Mount Wutai was also known as "cool mountain". When he heard about this, Emperor Wen of the Sui Dynasty issued an decree to build a temple on each of the five peaks to worship Manjusri Bodhisattva, "Intelligent Manjusri" (*Congming Wenshu*) on the east peak, "Lion Roaring Manjusri" (*Shizihou Wenshu*) on the west peak, "Wise Manjusri" (*Zhihui Wenshu*) on the south peak, "Clean Manjursi" (*Wugou Wenshu*) on the north peak and "Pure Manjursi" (*Rutong Wenshu*) on the central peak. Manjusri Bodhisattva then could see sunrise on the east peak, appreciate bright moon on the west peak, enjoy mountain flowers on the south peak and watch snow on the north peak. That tells the history of Mount Wutai.

- 明代铜镲金文殊菩萨像

  文殊菩萨是佛教四大菩萨之一，释迦牟尼佛的左胁侍菩萨，代表聪明智慧。

  Gilded Bronze Statue of Manjusri Bodhisattva of Ming Dynasty

  Manjusri Bodhisattva is one of the four great Buddha in Buddhism on the left side of Sakyamuni representing wisdom and intelligence.

佛光寺四绝
Four Wonders of Buddha's Light Temple (*Foguang Si*)

五台山的佛光寺有四绝，即东大殿内的唐木构、泥塑、壁画和墨迹。

There are four wonders in the Temple of Buddha's Light: wooden-frame structures of Tang Dynasty, clay statues, wall paintings and calligraphies.

唐木构

五台山佛光寺东大殿是唐代木结构建筑的典范。建筑庄重朴实，规模宏伟，细部构件精细，样式繁多，手法典型，是中国现存木结构建筑中使用最久的。

Wooden-frame Structures of the Tang Dynasty

The Eastern Great Hall in the temple represents the model of wooden building structures of the Tang Dynasty, which are simple, elegant, and magnificent with great varieties of exquisitely ornaments and building components. It is one of the wooden structures existing today in China that has been used the longest time in history.

泥塑

佛光寺东大殿有唐代彩塑30多尊，明代罗汉像296尊，造型精巧，工艺精湛，具有极高的艺术价值。

Clay Statues

The Eastern Great Hall has over 30 painted sculptures of the Tang Dynasty and 296 arhats sulpptures of the Ming Dynasty. It demonstrates exquisite craftsmanship and has a very high artistic values.

壁画

东大殿内槽拱眼壁有14幅唐代壁画，画中众位菩萨庄严宝相，慈悲虔诚，颇具唐画风韵。

Wall paintings

In the wall alcoves of the Eastern Great Hall display 14 Tang Dynasty wall paintings of different looks of Buddha demonstrating their benevolence, mercy and devotion. All retained the original style of paintings in the Tang Dynasty.

墨迹

殿内共有古人墨迹十余处，横跨唐、五代、金、元、明、清各个朝代，具有很高的欣赏价值和研究价值。

Calligraphies

A dozen of ancient calligraphies across the Tang, Five dynasties, Jing, Yuan, Ming and Qing dynasties can be seen in the Eastern Great Hall with very high research values. and appreciation value.

> 峨眉山

　　峨眉山位于中国四川省峨眉山市境内,景区面积154平方公里,以气势磅礴、雄秀幽奇的自然景色和浓厚的佛教文化氛围闻名于世。峨眉山是大峨山、二峨山、三峨山、四峨山的总称。其中,大峨山和二峨山遥遥相对,如同两条修长的眉毛,故称"峨眉山"。峨眉山地势复杂,山中峰峦叠嶂,沟壑纵横,奇石怪洞层出不穷,飞瀑流泉点缀山间。最高峰万佛顶海拔3099米,与峨眉平原2600多米的落差使得峨眉山横跨亚温带和寒温带,气象万千,形成了"一山有四季,十里不同天"的奇异景色。而山上3000多种植物和活泼灵动的猴群更是为峨眉山增添了生机和活力。

　　峨眉山优美的自然景观和良

> Mount Emei (*Emei Shan*)

Located within the boundaries of Emei Shan City, Sichuan Province, Mount Emei covers an area of 154 square kilometers famous for its magnificent and elegant natural scenery and rich Buddhist culture. Mount Emei is a mountain range comprising Mount Da'e, Mount Er'e, Mount San'e and Mount Si'e. It was named after two opposite mountains, Mount Da'e and Mount Er'e, whose contours resemble the image of two long and graceful eyebrows, hence the name Emei (*Mei* means eyebrow in Chinese). Its diverse topography includes undulating ridges, deep valleys and gullies, high peaks and strangely shaped rocks and caves with waterfalls and creeks in between. The highest peak, the Ten Thousand Buddha Summit (*Wanfo Ding*), is 3,099 meters above sea level. The altitude gap of 2,600 meters from

峨眉山风光
Scenery of Mount Emei

好的生态环境吸引了古今中外求仙修道的人们。相传峨眉山是佛教普贤菩萨的道场，至今山上都留有普贤菩萨的许多痕迹，如万年寺内普贤骑白象的铜像、普贤洗象池等。峨眉山最初曾是道教圣地，自隋唐佛教兴起后，逐渐取代了道教的地位，原有道观纷纷改成寺院。鼎盛时期，有寺庙170座，僧侣最多时达到3000人。近两千年的佛教发展历程，给峨眉山留下了丰富的佛教文化遗产，成就了许多高僧大德，使峨眉山逐步成为中国乃至世界影响深远的佛教圣地。1996年12月6日，峨眉山—乐山大佛作为一项文化与

the Emei plain brings Mount Emei a unique natural beauty and a unique climate across subtemperate and cold temperate zones, described as having "four seasons within one mountain and a different sky within ten miles." More than 3,000 plant species and lively monkeys give more vitality to Mount Emei.

Mount Emei's natural beauty and fine ecological environment have attracted visitors looking for immortality and self-cultivation from all over the world since ancient times. It is said that Mount Emei was the place of enlightenment for Bodhisattva Samantabhadra (*Puxian Pusa*). Many of his traces left behind still exist today including his statue riding a white elephant in the Ten Thousand-Year Temple (*Wannian Si*) and the pond where he washed his elephant. Mount Emei originally was a Taoist sacred site. As Buddhism became popular in the Sui and Tang dynasties, Buddhism took over the status of Taoism and Taoist sites were gradually changed to Buddhist temples. In the period of great prosperity, there were over 3,000 monks and 170 temples

自然双重遗产被联合国教科文组织列入《世界遗产名录》。

金顶

　　金顶为峨眉山主峰，海拔3077米。顶上有一个小平原。明朝万历年间妙峰禅师在此修建一座铜殿，被皇帝朱翊钧题名"永明华藏寺"。华藏寺在阳光照耀下光彩夺目，十分壮观，因此称为"金顶"。后经过失火重修，华藏寺更加轩昂宏伟、辉煌壮观。新金顶以

in Mount Emei. The development of Buddhism in nearly two thousand years left a rich cultural heritage of Buddhism in Mount Emei and brought about many noted Buddhist monks and their achievements. As a result Mount Emei became a Buddhist sacred site of great cultural significance and influence in China and abroad. On December 2nd, 1996 Mount Emei and the Great Buddha of Leshan were both added to the UNESCO World Heritage List for their natural and cultural heritage.

- 峨眉山金顶
  Golden Summit in Mount Emei

十方普贤铜像
Bronze Statue of Samantabhadra

Golden Summit (*Jin Ding*)

The Golden Summit is the main peak of Mount Emei at an altitude of 3077 meters with a flat area at the top. The Zen master Miaofeng monk of the Ming Dynasty built a bronze hall and later was named by Emperor Zhu Xujun as the *Yongming Huazang* Temple. Under the sunshine, the temple is dazzling and magnificent, hence the name Golden Summit Temple (*Jinding Si*). It was rebuilt after being destroyed by fire. The Golden Summit now looks even more spectacular with the statue of Samantabhadra in the center and the Golden Hall, Bronze Hall and Silver Hall along the pilgrimage boulevard. Standing next to the precipitous Self-Sacrifice Cliff (*Sheshen Yan*) at this high altitude, beautiful scenery can be seen in all directions providing a full enjoyment whether to watch the sunrise, the sea of clouds, the Buddha's light or thousands of floating orbs of light at night.

The bronze statue of Samantabhadra is 48 meters high and weighs a total of 660 tons. It is the highest gold Buddha statue in the world. Forty-eight meters represents forty-eight wishes of height. Samantabhadra's ten heads are placed

十方普贤铜像为中心，由金殿、铜殿、银殿和朝圣大道组成。这里地势高耸、景色壮美，站在陡峭的舍身岩边，四方的琼山秀水一览无余，观日出、望云海、看佛光、赏圣灯，乃人生一大乐事。

殿外的普贤铜像，通高48米，总重量达660吨，是世界上最高的金佛。金佛通高48米，代表的是阿弥陀佛的48个愿望。普贤菩萨的十个头像分为三层，神态各异，代表了世人的十种心态。四面刻有普贤菩萨的十种广大行愿。

separately in three levels representing ten states of mind of human beings. Samantabhadra's ten great vows are inscribed on the four sides of the statue.

峨眉山金顶的三大奇观
Three Wonders of the Mount Emei's Golden Summit

峨眉金顶山高云低，景色壮美秀丽，有云海、佛光、圣灯三大自然奇观。

The spectacular view at the Mount Emei's Golden Summit is magnificent and elegant with soaring mountains and clouds floating urderfoot. It displays three natural wonders: the sea of clouds, the Buddha' light and divine lights.

云海

每当峨眉山晴空万里时，白云从千山万壑间冉冉升起，一时间就会形成苍茫的云海，好像雪白的绒毯一样平铺在地面上，望不到边际。人站在云层之间，仿佛升仙一般。云海一出现，峨眉山的千山万壑都被掩藏得无影无踪。最为壮观的是，如果大风骤起，云海就会随风卷起云浪或云柱，时而腾空跃起，时而徐徐散落，瞬息万变。

Sea of Clouds

When Mount Emei has a bright sky, white clouds can rise up slowly from ridges and gorges and then quickly form a sea of clouds as if it was a white carpet unfolding on the ground stretching out endlessly. When standing in the middle of the clouds and mists one feels like ascending to the sky like a fairy. When the sea of clouds appears, all ridges and gorges seem to hide away without a trace. The most enthralling phenomenon happens when a strong wind surges suddenly and the sea of clouds will change rapidly by the minute, sometimes flowing up like a cloud pillar or high waves and sometimes scattering slowly all over the mountain.

佛光

每当峨眉山弥漫着大雾时，如果人背对着太阳，站在金顶上，阳光就会从身后射过来。这时，在不远处的雾幕上，会映出一个彩虹般的光环，中间清晰呈现那人的影子，并且影随人动、形影不离，这就是峨眉山的又一大奇观——"佛光"。即使有成百上千人同时背对太阳，每个人也只能看到自己的身影被光环笼罩，十分神奇。其实，"佛光"是光的一种自然现象，因阳光照射雾气表面而形成。

Buddha Light
When Mount Emei immerses in a dense fog, if one stands with the back against the sun at the top of the Golden Summit and the sun shines through misty clouds, the person's shadow can be seen in the foggy sky outlined by iridescent light. The light moves along with the moving shadow. Even if hundreds or thousands of people stand between the sun and the clouds, each will only see his/her own

• 《峨眉金顶图轴》（现代 张大千）
Scroll Painting of the Golden Summit of Mount Emei by Zhang Daqian, Modern

shadow outlined by Buddha's light. The amazing light has become a wonder of Mount Emei. In fact, the Buddha light is a natural phenomenon caused by sun shining through the misty clouds.

圣灯

每当黑夜降临，而天空中又没有月亮，金顶的舍身岩下就会出现飘浮的绿色光团，从一点、两点形成千万点，好像群星闪烁，又像是无数灯光时暗时亮，因此被人们称为"圣灯"。圣灯其实也是一种自然现象，但专家们对此却有着不同的解释，普遍认为这是山谷的磷火燃起，还有人说是一些树木上的一种蜜环菌，当空气达到一定湿度时发光所致。

Divine Lights
At night when the moon is waning, people looking down from the Self-Sacrifice Cliff at Golden Summit can see thousands of floating orbs of green lights like shining stars. Sometimes they look darker and sometimes they look brighter. People called them "divine lights". In fact it is a natural phenomenon. Scientists have different explanations. Some said that this is caused by phosphine from animal decomposition and some said that the glow is from armillaria grown on trees when humidity in the air reaches certain level.

万年寺

万年寺是峨眉山历史最久的古刹之一，创建于东晋，时名"普贤寺"，唐僖宗时慧通禅师重建，更名"白水寺"。明代万历皇帝朱翊钧题赠"圣寿万年寺"，简称"万年寺"，为峨眉山最早的六大古寺之一。万年寺踞观心岭下，门迎大坪寺、牛心寺等寺和石笋峰、钵盂峰诸峰，海拔1020米，因供奉普贤

Ten Thousand-Year Temple (*Wannian Si*)

The Ten Thousand-Year Temple (*Wannian Si*) has the longest history of all ancient temple in Mount Emei. Built in the Eastern Jin Dynasty (317-420) it was called "Samantabhadra Temple" originally and changed to "the White Water Temple" when it was rebuilt by Monk Huitong in Tang Dynasty (618-907). Emperor Zhu Yujun of the Ming

• 峨眉山万年寺 (图片提供：全景正片)
Ten Thousand-Year Temple in Mount Emei

铜像而驰名。万年寺的寺院布局十分精美，整座寺院坐西朝东，依次为山门、弥勒殿、砖殿、巍峨宝殿、大雄宝殿。全寺除砖殿为砖石穹隆顶外，其余均为木结构，是峨眉山规模最大的寺庙。其中第二殿圆顶方形，除大门外不用一梁一木，故名"无梁殿"。万年寺历史悠久，高僧辈出，佛教文物十分丰富，各种佛像、法器、书画、匾对、寺院建筑、寺院装饰都展现出极高的艺术品位。唐代开元年间，诗人李白来游峨眉山时，住在万年

Dynasty inscribed "the Divine Longevity of Ten Thousand-Year Temple" (abbreviated "the Ten Thousand-Year Temple"). It was one of the six earliest temples in Mount Emei. At 1,020 meters above sea level, the temple is situated at the foot of the Contemplation Summit (*Guanxin Ling*) facing the Flat Ground Temple (Daping Si), Cattle Heart Temple (*Niuxin Si*), Stalagmite Summit (*Shisun Feng*) and *Bomeng* Summit in the front. It is well known for its bronze statue of Samantabhadra Buddha. As the largest tepmle in Mount Emei, the entire complex faces the west and has an exquisite layout

寺毗卢殿，听广浚和尚弹琴，写下了许多名诗。万年寺风景优美，特别是秋高气爽之时，红枫、银杏色彩绚烂，层林尽染的秋色倒影在碧波盈盈的池水之中，这富有诗意的风光被誉为峨眉山十景之一——"白水秋风"。

清音阁

清音阁又名"卧云寺"，位于峨眉山牛心岭下黑白二水汇流处，海拔710米，由唐僖宗年间慧通禅师修建，寺内供有释迦牟尼、文殊、普贤大师之像。清音阁景色优美，意境深远。黑、白双水交汇于形如牛心的黑色巨石处，水石撞击，清脆作响，水面架有两座浮桥如同鸟翼飞翎，称"双飞桥"，构成了峨眉山十景之一——"双桥清音"。更有人将这亭台楼阁与宜人景色的天然结合誉为"峨眉山第一风景"。

in the order of the front gate, Maitreya Hall (*Mile Dian*), Brick Hall, Majestic Hall (*Weier Baodian*) and Mahavira Hall (*Daxiongbao Dian*). Except for the Brick Hall with a brick arch roof, all other halls are wooden structures. Maitreya Hall (*Mile Dian*) is also called the Beamless Hall because except for the gate not a single piece of wood beam was used. The temple has a long history having many notable senior monks in residence and possesses a rich collection of Buddhist relics including Buddha statues, Buddhist instruments, calligraphies, paintings, Tablet couplets, Buddhist architectural decorations, all showing very high level of artistic taste. Li Bai, a famous poet of the Tang Dynasty stayed in Buddha Losana Hall (*Pilu Dian*) and wrote many well-known poems while listening to the music played by Guangjun Monk. In the fall when Mount Emei enjoys the best weather, the mountain range is decorated with colorful maple and ginkgo trees reflected on the green water lake. This poetic scenery is called "White Water in the Wind of Fall" and considered one of the ten best sceneries in Mount Emei.

Clear Sound Tower (*Qingyin Ge*)

The Clear Sound Tower (*Qingyin Ge*), also known as Seclusion Temple (*Woyun Si*), is situated at the foot of the Cattle Heart Summit (*Niuxin Ling*) between a stream of darker brook and crystal brook at an altitude of 710 meters. It was constructed by Huitong Monk between the year of 873 and 888 in the Tang Dynasty. Inside enshrines the statues of Sakyamuni, Manjusri, Samantabhadra Buddha. Surrounded by an enchanting environment, the dark and crystal brooks converge at a huge black rock with a cattle heart shape making a clear and crisp sound. There are two floating bridges over the streams looking like flying birds, hence the name "Double Flying Bridges". The sound of the water and the bridge became one of the ten best sceneries of Mount Emei known as "Double Bridges with Clear Sound". Some people even laud this perfect match between pavilions and natural scenery as the "No. 1 Scenic Beauty of Mount Emei."

• 峨眉山清音阁牛心亭 (图片提供：FOTOE)
Cattle Heart Pavilion of Clear Sound Tower in Mount Emei

峨眉山月歌（唐 李白）

峨眉山月半轮秋，影入平羌江水流。

夜发清溪向三峡，思君不见下渝州。

诗词译文：

　　峨眉山的秋月，犹如一弯琼舟，航行在天空，月光倒映在嘉陵江中。

　　我乘舟离开清溪驶向三峡，本想与你道别，可你没有来。我只好悻悻地顺流而下回重庆了。

Song of Moon in Mount Emei by Li Bai, Tang Dynasty (618-907)

Poem Interpretation

The fall moon in Mount Emei like a crescent-shaped jade plate sails in the sky with the moonlight reflecting in the Jialing River;

I am riding the boat leaving Qingxi for the Three Gorges, wishing to say farewell to you; but you didn't come and I have to go downstream to Chongqing in a bitter mood.

> 九华山

　　九华山坐落在安徽省青阳县城西南20公里处，方圆120公里，主峰十王峰海拔1342米。九华山原名"九子山"，后因李白"妙有分二气，灵山开九华"的佳句而改名为"九华山"。九华山山水雄奇灵秀，九十九峰其型各异，风光无限，其中十王、天柱、天台、莲花、罗汉、芙蓉、独秀等九峰因形似莲花而闻名天下。山中地势险要，悬崖沟壑无一不精妙险峻，古洞怪石无一不鬼斧神工，参天古树、翠郁山竹、溪泉瀑布韵味幽远，名胜古迹若隐若现，"五溪山色""天台晓日""平岗积雪""天柱仙迹"等景观如梦如幻，犹如世外桃源般，故而被誉为"东南第一山"。

> **Mount Jiuhua (*Jiuhua Shan*)**

Mount Jiuhua (*Jiuhua Shan*), 20 kilometers southwest of Qingyang County, Anhui Province, covers an area of 120 square kilometers with the main peak "Ten King Peak" (*Shiwang Feng*) at 1,342 meters above sea level. Originally Mount Jiuhua was named Mount Jiuzi (*Jiuzi Shan*). Later it was changed to Mount Jiuhua meaning Mountain of the Nine Blossoms based on a poem by poet Li Bai of the Tang Dynasty. The marvelous landscape of Mount Jiuhua shows off the different shapes of the ninety-nine high peaks, of which the Ten Kings (*Shiwang*), the Celestial Pillar (*Tianzhu*), the Celestial Terrace (*Tiantai*), the Lotus Flower(*Lianhua*), the Arhats (*Luohan*), the Lotus(*Furong*), the Unique Beauty (*Duxiu*) are well-known for their resemblance of lotus flowers. Mount Jiuhua has a fame as the "No. 1 Mountain in the Southeast" for its precipitous ridges, gorges and gullies,

九华山不仅自然风光迷人，佛教人文景观更是九华山的名片。根据记载，早在唐天宝年间，新罗国王的近亲金乔觉曾在九华山上潜心修持，后被众佛徒认定为地藏菩萨的化身，九华山由此被辟为地藏道场。此后九华山香火鼎盛，寺庙林立，浓厚的佛教氛围与山中锦绣风光自然融合，成为中国四大佛教名山之一。

grotesque caves and rocks, towering ancient pines, gorgeous bamboos, deep quiet creeks and waterfalls, and cultural relics scattered in the mountain. There are some fairyland-like scenery such as "Five Streams in Mountain Color", "Celestial Terrace for the Rising Sun", "Snow Piling on Flat Ridge" and "Celestial Pillar with Immortal Footprints".

In addition to its natural scenic beauty, Mount Jiuhua is one of the most important shrines of Buddhist culture and civilization.

大诗人李白

李白是唐代伟大的浪漫主义诗人，存世诗文千余篇，代表作有《蜀道难》《行路难》《将进酒》等。李白的诗雄奇飘逸，俊逸清新，富有浪漫主义精神，被称为"诗仙"。他在诗中，常常讴歌祖国山河与美丽的自然风光，借以抒发内心的强烈情感，同时也展现了他洒脱不羁的气质和傲世独立的人格。

The Great Poet Li Bai

Li Bai was a great poet of Romanticism in the Tang Dynasty (581-618). He left behind thousands of poems and verses. Some of his masterpieces include "Hard Roads in Shu" (*Shudao Nan*), "The Hard Road" (*Xinglu Nan*) and "Bringing In the Wine" (*Qiang Jinjiu*). He was called "Immortal Poet" because of his poetry style of imagery of fantasy and romanticism as well as technical virtuosity. He often expressed in his poems his strong feelings and demonstrated uninhibited temperament and independent personality through eulogizing mountains, rivers and natural landscape.

李白像
Portrait of Li Bai

九华山风光 (图片提供：全景正片)
Scenery of Mount Jiuhua

化城寺

化城寺为开山祖寺，南望芙蓉峰，东临东崖，西有神光岭，北倚白云山，四山环绕如城。化城寺坐北朝南，中轴线分别为灵官殿、天王殿、大雄宝殿、藏经楼，其藏经楼建于明朝，内藏完好的明朝《涅槃经》，明代无瑕和尚曾刺血书写

According to historical records, Jin Qiaoque, a close relative of the Silla king came to Mount Jiuhua and cultivated himself between the year of 742 and 756 in the Tang Dynasty. He was thought to be the incarnation of Ksitigarbha Buddha and as a result Mount Jiuhua became a Buddhist sacred site. Since then, Buddhist activities flourished in Mount Jiuhua. With the natural scenic beauty emerged with rich Buddhist culture, Mount Jiuhua is one of the four most famous Buddhist sacred mountains in China.

Huacheng Temple

Huacheng Temple is the founding ancestral temple in Mount Jiuhua. Surrounding the complex like fortresses are four mountain peaks: the Lotus Peak (*Ferong Feng*) in the south, East Cliff (*Dong Ya*) in the east, the Divine Light Summit (*Shenguang Ling*) in the west and the White Cloud Mountain (*Baiyun Shan*) in the north. The entire temple faces south with the Celestial Palace Hall (*Linggong Dian*), Heavenly King Hall (*Tianwang Dian*), Mahavira Hall (*Daxiong Baodian*) and the Sutra Hall

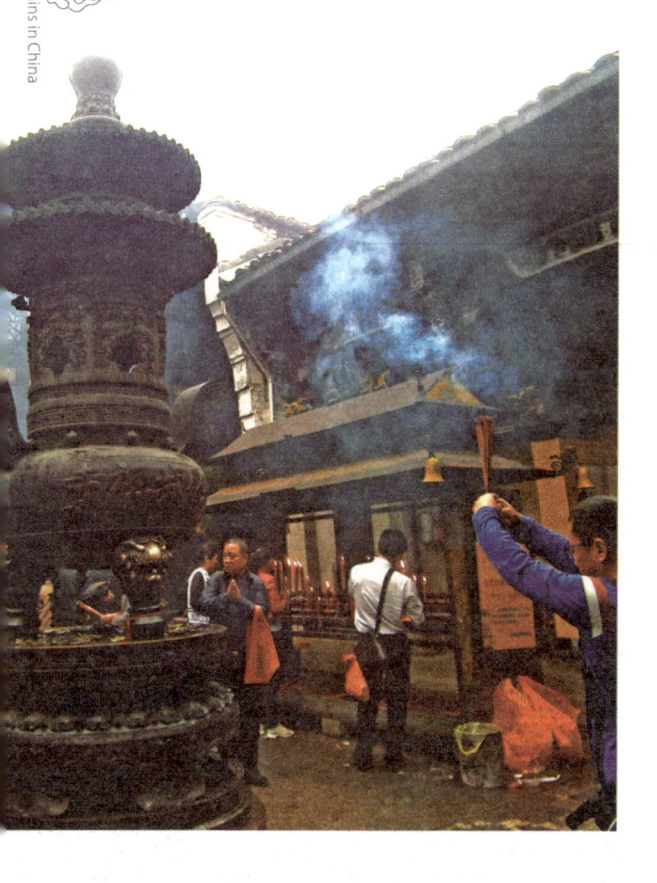

• 九华山化城寺 (图片提供：FOTOE)
Huacheng Temple in Mount Jiuhua

《华严经》。殿内有清代康熙皇帝御书"九华圣境"横匾和乾隆御书"芬陀普教"横匾。后殿挂明代崇祯皇帝御书"为善最乐"横匾。寺内原有一座万余斤的古钟，现存的铜钟重1000公斤，高约2米，铸于清光绪年间，制作精美，音质洪亮悠扬。每当黄昏时分，化城寺钟声一响，全山寺院僧尼随钟声开始诵经。寺庙内击鼓鸣磬，木鱼声、僧尼诵经声，婉转悠扬。每逢新年伊始，撞钟108响，代表12个月、24个节气、72候，意味着岁岁平安，时时报喜，消灾灭祸。

肉身殿

肉身殿坐落于化城寺以西的神光岭上，是朝拜地藏的重要场所。相传唐玄宗时，新罗僧人金乔觉来华求法，于此山无人处择一岩洞栖居修行。唐贞元十年（794年），99岁的金乔觉圆寂，其肉身置函中经三年，仍"颜色如生"，众佛徒认定他即地藏菩萨示现，遂建一石塔将其肉身供于石塔中，尊为"金地藏"，后又在宽阔的塔基上兴建庙宇，称"肉身殿"。肉身殿是塔

(*Cangjing Lou*) along the central axis of the complex. Built during the Ming Dynasty (1368-1644), the Sutra Hall stores the well-preserved "Nirvana Sutra" and "Avatamsaka Sutra" written by Monk Wuxia with his own blood in the Ming Dynasty. The temple also houses the "Jiuhua Sacred Site" tablet personally inscribed by Emperor Kangxi of the Qing Dynasty, the "Fragrant Grand Temple" tablet inscribed by Emperor Qianlong of the Qing Dynasty and the "Kindness is Happiness" tablet inscribed by Emperor Chongzhen of the Ming Dynasty in the back hall. Inside the temple there used to be an ancient bell that weighed over 5000 kilograms. The extant bronze bell, cast between 1875 and 1908 in the Qing Dynasty,weighs about 1000 kilograms at 2 meters high. The bell has a superior craftsmanship and a resonant melodious sound. Every day at dusk when the bell rings, monks and nuns start beating drums and wooden fish (a Buddhist praying instrument), and chanting sutra along with the ringing bell. At the beginning of a new year, the bell rings 108 times representing 12 months, 24 Chinese solar terms and 72 *Hou* (an ancient Chinese time unit; every 3 *Hou* comes a Chinese solar terms), which signify peace for all,

殿式建筑，建于高台之上，石柱、红墙、铁瓦、汉白玉铺地，氛围庄严，气魄非凡。正门高悬"东南

九华山肉身殿 (图片提供：FOTOE)
The Body Hall of Mount Jiuhua

good fortune and prevention of evils and bad luck for the year.

Body Hall (*Roushen Dian*)

The Body Hall (*Roushen Dian*), an important site to worship Ksitigarbha Buddha, is located at the Devine Light Summit (*Shenguang Ling*) west of the *Huacheng* Temple. It is said that during the Tang Dynasty, Silla monk Jin Qiaojue came to China to seek enlightenment through Buddhist practices and he chose a cave in Mount Jiuhua for his self-cultivation. In the year of 794 he died at the age of 99. When his body was found in the cave three years later, he still had life-like color. Monks on Mount Jiuhua believed that he was the reincarnation of Ksitigarbha Buddha, so they built a stone pagoda to house his body and named it "Golden Ksitigarbha". Later a temple was built on the spacious foundation of the pagoda and was named "the Body Hall". The Body Hall also has a pagoda architecture built with stone pillars, red walls, and iron-cast tiles. The ground is covered with white marble and it makes the hall magnificent. Over the main entrance door, there is a tablet inscribed "No. 1 Mountain in South-east China."

第一山"匾额。殿中央七层木结构的地藏塔,塔基用汉白玉砌成。塔内供奉一百多尊地藏菩萨,正面供金地藏塑像。塔的前后安置着大大小小的地藏塑像,两侧是十殿阎罗拱卫而立。寺内文物众多,琳琅满目,不胜枚举。

祇园寺

祇园寺位于九华街入口处,建筑面积5157平方米。祇园寺的名字取自佛经故事——相传释迦牟尼在佛教圣地祇园宣扬佛教二十余年。祇园寺始建于明嘉靖年间,是九华山唯一一座宫殿式庙宇,庙宇错落有致,结构精巧,气势宏大。主要由灵官殿、弥勒殿、大雄宝殿、客堂、斋堂、库院、退居寮、方丈寮和光明讲堂等9座单体建筑组成。步入寺门,穿过天王殿,大雄宝殿内供奉着三尊大佛,各高3丈,是九华山最高的佛像。大佛两侧有十八罗汉和佛教浮雕,整个殿堂宝气庄严,金碧辉煌。大殿前有法堂、禅堂,北边有斋堂、衣钵寮、云水寮等楼院。其中厨房内存7口铜质大锅,最大的一口直径173厘米,高56

In the center of the hall is the 7-story wooden pagoda of Ksitigarbha Buddha with a white marble base. Over one hundred statues of Ksitigarbha Buddha are enshrined inside of the pagoda. The gold statue of Ksitigarbha Buddha is set in the center and it is surrounded by many different sizes of Buddha along with ten Yama guards. There are numerous cultural relics displayed inside the hall.

Qiyuan Temple

Qiyuan Temple is at the entrance of the Jiuhua Street in an area of 5,157 square meters. The name Qiyuan came from a story in the Buddhist sutra, which says that Sakyamuni advocated Buddhism in the sacred site of Qiyuan for over twenty years. The temple was first built during the Ming Dynasty (1368-1644) and is the only temple of an imperial palace style. The layout of the complex is monumental and elegant consisting mainly of nine structures including Celestial Hall (*Linggong Dian*), Maitreya Hall (*Mile Dian*), Mahavira Hall (*Daxiong Baodian*), the Guess House, the Buddhist Fasting House, the Storage Courtyard, the Seclusive House, the Abbot House and the Brightness Preaching Hall

厘米，人称"千僧灶"，一次可煮米200公斤。寺庙东南方向是光明讲堂和藏经阁，其中藏经阁内收藏

(*Guangming Jiangtang*). Stepping into the temple's gate and walking through the Heavenly King Hall(*Tianwang Dian*). There are three statues of Buddha setting in this resplendent and magnificent Mahavira Hall, which are the biggest statues of Buddha in Mount Jiuhua, each ten meters high with eighteen Arhat

● 九华山祇园寺（图片提供：全景正片）
　Qiyuan Temple in Mount Jiuhua

有清代唯一的官刻汉文大藏经《龙藏》和1669部经书。整个建筑依山就势，鳞次栉比，巧妙融于自然山水之间，肃穆壮观的建筑和青松绿水相偎相依，意蕴深远，引人入胜。

statues and Buddhist embossments on both sides. There are the preaching room and cultivation room at the front of the Mahavira Hall with the fasting room, dressing room and wandering house to the north. The temple's kitchen keeps seven bronze cauldrons, the largest having 173 centimeters in diameter and 56 centimeters in height, which are known as "thousand monks cauldrons" for its capacity of cooking 200 kilograms of rice each time. The Brightness Preaching Hall and the Sutra Library are in the southeast area of the temple. The library has the only Tripitaka collection in Chinese printed by the Qing imperial court and 1,669 other Tripitaka books. The entire temple structure follows the topology of mountains and valleys integrating the beautiful landscape of forests and water, which perfectly integrates the nature and the architecture in one complex.

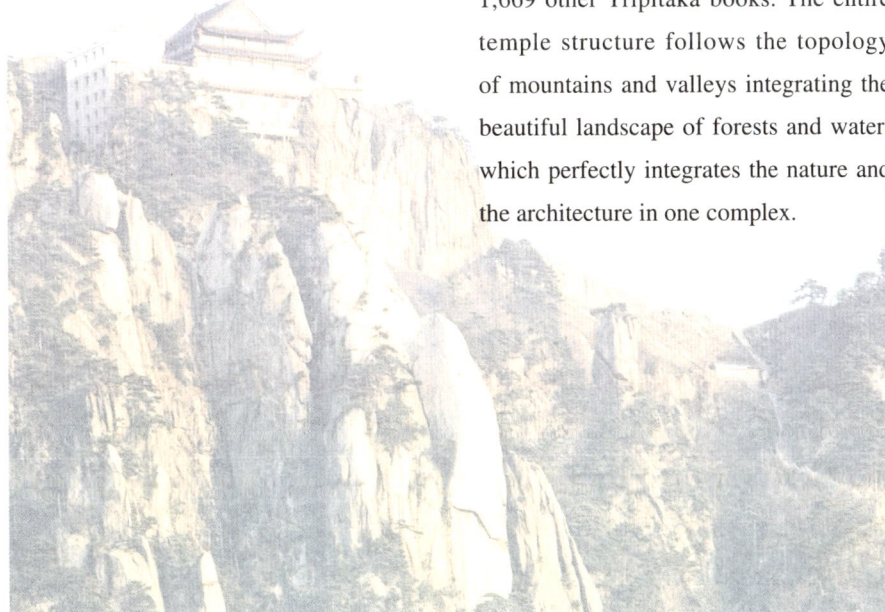

> 普陀山

普陀山位于浙江省杭州湾以东100海里的莲花洋中，是舟山群岛1390个岛屿中的一个小岛。小岛南北狭长，面积近13平方公里，四面环海。特殊的地理位置为普陀山蒙上了一层神秘而又神圣的面纱。古有诗称"海上有仙山，山在虚无缥缈间"。岛上风景旖旎，山峦起伏，最高峰佛山顶海拔290米，为全岛之巅。普陀山上的奇峰、怪石、古洞与海边的风景相映成趣，海天一色之美景随处可见，素有"南海圣境"之称。

早在东晋时，就有喜好修道的葛洪（著名道教学者、医药学家）前来炼丹。唐朝时，普陀山开始成为供奉观音的佛地，鼎盛时码头香船林立，前来朝拜求法的信徒络绎

> Mount Putuo (*Putuo Shan*)

Mount Putuo (*Putuo Shan*) is situated in a small islet in the Lotus Sea (*Lianhua Yang*) 100 nautical miles east of Hangzhou Bay, Zhejiang Province. Among 1,390 islets in the Zhoushan islands, this narrow islet stretches from south to north covering an area of 13 square kilometers surrounded by the sea. This special geological position gives a mysterious and sacred veil to Mount Putuo described in the ancient poem as "the celestial mountain on the sea, a mountain of illusion". The islet has stunning scenery and rolling hills. The highest peak in Mount Putuo is the Buddha Mountain Summit (*Foshan Ding*) at 290 meters above sea level. Peculiarly shaped peaks and rocks, ancient caverns and beaches on the island all come together as one scenic beauty known as "the Sacred Site of the South Sea".

● 普陀山风光 (图片提供: 全景正片)
Scenery of Mount Putuo

不绝。曾有三大寺，八十八庵，一百二十八茅蓬，号称"五百丛林，三千僧众"。目前尚有普济、法雨、慧济三大寺和大乘、梅福、紫竹林等三十余座禅院供人朝圣、观光。

观音菩萨是很多中国百姓崇奉的菩萨。菩萨端庄慈祥，手持净瓶杨柳，过去人们相信，观音菩萨具

As early as in the Eastern Jin Dynasty (317-420), Ge Hong, a well known Taoist scholar, and a Chinese medicine expert, came to Mount Putuo to make elixir for immortality. Starting from the Tang Dynasty (618-907), Mount Putuo became a Buddhist sacred site for worshipping Bodhisattva Guanyin. At the height of its popularity, many boats docked at the pier filled with Buddhist pilgrims. There

• 《观音图》（宋 法常）

Portrait of Bodhisattva Guanyin by Fa Chang, Southern Song Dynasty (1127-1279)

有无量的智慧和神通，大慈大悲，普救人间疾苦。

普济禅寺

　　普济禅寺是供奉观音的主刹，有"五步一楼，十步一阁"之称，是岛上第一大寺。普济禅寺创建于唐咸通年间，后宋神宗于1080年将

were once three big monasteries, eighty-eight converts and one hundred and twenty-eight Buddhist cottages carrying a reputation of "three thousand monks in five hundred temples". Today, over thirty Buddhist structures are open to tourists including the three big temples of Universal Relief (*Puji*), Buddhadharma (*Fayu*) and *Huiji* as well as smaller temples such as Mahayana (*Dacheng*), *Meifu* Deity and Purple Bamboo Forest (*Zizhu Lin*), etc.

　　Bodhisattva Guanyin has many believers. Guanyin holds in one of hands a pure bottle inserted with willow branches. People in the past believed Guanyin has mighty wisdom, supernatural power and great compassion to achieve salvation for mankind.

Universal Relief Zen Temple (*Puji Chansi*)

Universal Relief Zen Temple (*Puji Chansi*) is the main and the biggest temple which enshrines Bodhisattva Guanyin on the Mount Putuo island. It has a reputation of "one pagoda every five steps and one pavilion every ten steps". It was first built between the year of 860 and 874 during the Tang Dynasty. Later in 1080 Emperor Shenzong of the Song Dynasty changed its name to "*Baotuo Guanyin*

普陀山普济禅寺
Universal Relief Zen Temple (*Puji Chansi*) in Mount Putuo

其改名为"宝陀观音寺",专供观音菩萨,香火始盛。到了南宋嘉定年间,被御赐"圆通宝殿"匾额,指定普陀山为专供观音的道场,与其后锦屏山下的法雨禅寺、法顶山上的慧济禅寺构成普陀山的主要观音道场,成为普陀山最主要的人文景观。普济禅寺有大圆通殿、天王殿、藏经楼等著名建筑。大圆通殿

Temple" to only worship Bodhisattva Guanyin and the temple started to became a popular Buddhist site. Between the year of 1208 and 1224 during the Southern Song Dynasty, a tablet inscribed with "Hall of Imperial Fund" (*Yuantong Baodian*) was bestowed by the imperial court. At the same period, Mount Putuo together with Temple of Buddhadharma (*Fayu Si*) at the foot of Jinping Mountain and Huji Temple (*Huiji Si*) at the top of the mountain constitued as Buddhist sacred sites dedicated solely to Bodhisattva Guanyin. All these places are considered the most important sites of Chinese civilizations and culture in Mount Putuo. Inside the temple, there are well-known buildings including the Hall of Grand Imperial Fund (*Dayuantong Dian*), Hall of Heavenly King (*Tianwang Dian*) and Sutras Library. The main hall in the temple is the Hall of Grand Imperial Fund, which houses an 8.8 meters high statue of the Vairocana Buddha with another 16 statues of different forms of Bodhisattva Guanyin, known as the "thirty-two incarnations of Bodhisattva Guanyin".

Buddhadharma Temple (*Fayu Si*)

Buddhadharma Temple (*Fayu Si*), 2.8 kilometers from the Universal Relief Zen

是全寺主殿，人称"活大殿"，供奉着高8.8米的毗卢观音，两壁各有16尊不同造型的观音菩萨，称"观音三十二应身"。

法雨禅寺

法雨禅寺又称"后寺"，距普济禅寺2.8公里，为普陀三大寺之一。法雨寺创建于明万历八年

Temple, is one of the three big temples in Mount Putuo. It was founded in 1580 during the Ming Dynasty covering an area of 33,408 square meters. The 294 extant structures built on six terraces following the terrain of the mountain. It has the meaning of climbing up to the Buddhist heaven one step at a time. Aligned on the central axis are the Hall of Heavenly King (*Tianwang Dian*), the Bell Tower, Jade Buddha Hall (*Yufo Dian*), Bodhisattva Guanyin Hall (*Guanyin Dian*), Imperial Tablet Hall (*Yubei Dian*), Mahavira Hall *(Daxiong Baodian)*, the Sutras Library (*Cangjing*

• 普陀山法雨禅寺 (图片提供：FOTOE)
Buddhadharma Temple (*Fayu Si*) in Mount Putuo

存殿宇209间，依山取势，分列亮层台基逐级升高，有步步升上佛国天堂之意。中轴线上有天王殿，后有玉佛殿，两殿之间有钟鼓楼，玉佛殿后依次为观音殿、御碑殿、大雄宝殿、藏经楼、方丈殿。观音殿又称"九龙殿"，殿中九龙壁用青石浮雕而成，工艺精美，栩栩如生，拆自明朝故宫九龙殿，是中国佛教建筑规格较高的佛殿，被誉为普陀山三宝之一。殿中供奉观音菩萨，两旁列有十八罗汉。整座寺庙宝相庄严，雄伟壮观，与灿烂的金沙海岸遥相呼应，每日间钟鼓声鸣和着阵阵涛声。

慧济禅寺

慧济禅寺位于海拔291.3米的佛顶山上，佛顶山又名"菩萨顶"，是普陀山的最高处。慧济禅寺因处于佛顶山中间的谷地，因而俗称"佛顶山寺"，为普陀山第三大寺。慧济禅寺原为一石亭，供佛其中，明代高僧慧圆创慧济庵，至清乾隆五十八年（1793年）始建圆通

Led and the Hall of Abbots (*Fangzhang Dian*). The Bodhisattva Guanyin Hall is also called the Nine Dragon Hall (*Jiulong Dian*), in which nine life-like dragons are embossed on bluestone with exquisite craftsmanship. The entire piece came from the nine dragon palace in the Forbidden City during the Ming Dynasty. The Bodhisattva Guanyin Hall ranks in high architectural status of Buddhist temples. It is acclaimed as one of the three treasures of Mount Putuo. The statue of Bodhisattva Guanyin is enshrined in the center with eighteen abbots lining up on both sides. The entire temple shows solemnity and sublimity echoed in the sound of bell ringing and bursts of waves in the nearby Golden Sand Beach (*Jinsha Haian*).

Huiji Temple

Huiji Temple is at the top of the Buddha Sumnuut mountain, also known as the "Bodhisattva Summit" at an altitude of 291.3 meters, the highest point in Mount Putuo. It is commonly called it the Buddha Summit Mountain Temple and it is the third largest temple in Mount Poutuo. Originally it was just a stone pagoda with a Buddhist statue inside. From the Ming Dynasty when it was first

殿、玉泉殿、大悲楼等，扩庵为寺。光绪三十三年（1907年），为了安放佛教典籍《大藏经》，增扩此寺，遂成巨刹。慧济禅寺布局独特，主要建筑均在一条平行线上，颇具浙东园林建筑风格。大雄宝殿供奉着释迦牟尼佛像，屋顶用天蓝、淡绿、鹅黄、紫红等色琉璃瓦盖成，阳光下映出万道"彩虹"，形成"佛光普照"的绚丽景象。观音殿建于1989年，汇集了根据唐、宋、元、明、清以来历代画家所绘观音像而镌的石刻观音共123尊，是普陀山宗教艺术的精华之一。寺院深藏于高岗林屏之中，错落有致的殿宇、曲折幽深的甬道营造出佛门特有的氛围。

constructed by the noted monk Huiyuan. Late till 1793 in the Qing Dynasty, structures such as the Imperial Fund Hall (*Yuantong Dian*), Jade Spring Hall (*Yuquan Dian*) and Compassion Hall (*Dabei Lou*) were built to expand the complex. In 1907, the Buddhist classic Tripitaka was placed here and the temple became one of the largest in Mount Poutuo. It has a unique layout with all major structures built along a horizontal line, a typical landscape architectural style in the east of Zhejiang Province. The Mahavira Hall enshrines the statue of Sakyamuni. The roof is covered with glazed tiles in sky blue, light green, light yellow and mauve colors, which reflect a iridescent shine under the sun commonly called "the Illuminating Buddha Light". The Hall of Bodhisattva Guanyin, constructed in 1989, houses 123 stone carved statues of Guanyin Bodhisattva based on paintings from famous painters of the Tang, Song, Yuan, Ming and Qing dynasties. They are considered parts of Buddhist art essence in Mount Putao. The temple is hidden deeply in the forests with well-designed layouts of Buddhist buildings and carefully mapped walkways in between creating a typical Buddhist atmosphere.

道教名山
Famous Taoist Mountains

　　道教是中国本土的一种宗教，距今已有1800余年的历史。中国有四大道教名山，即武当山、青城山、齐云山和龙虎山。

Taoism is an indigenous religion in China with a history of over 1,800 years. There are four famous Taoist mountains: Mount Wudang (*Wudang Shan*), Mount Qincheng (*Qincheng Shan*), Mount Qiyun (*Qiyun Shan*) and Mount Longhu (*Longhu Shan*, literally Mount Dragon and Tiger).

> 武当山

　　武当山又名"玄岳山""太和山"，位于湖北省十堰市丹江口境内，是中国著名的道教圣地之一。武当山北临丹江口水库，南接神农架山区，西连秦岭，东迤大洪山，方圆400公里，古代号称"八百里武当"，可见其规模的宏大。武当山风景兼泰山之伟、黄山之奇、雁荡之幽，北宋大书画家米芾将之誉为"天下第一山"。武当山峰峦清秀，风景幽邃，以天柱峰为中心，有上、下十八盘等险道、"七十二峰朝大顶"和"金殿叠影"等景观。主峰天柱峰，海拔1612米，被誉为"一柱擎天"。四周南岩峰、双笔峰、玉女峰、望郎峰、仙人峰等向主峰倾斜，形成"万山来朝"的奇观。

> Mount Wudang (*Wudang Shan*)

Mount Wudang (*Wudang Shan*), also known as "Mount Xuanyue" (*Xuanyue Shan*) and "Mount Supreme Harmony" (*Taihe Shan*), is situated in Danjiangkou County of Shiyan City, Hubei Province. It is one of the major Taoist sacred sites in China. It covers an area of 400 square kilometers with the Danjiangkou Reservoir to the north, Shennongjia Natural Reserve to the south, Qinling Mountains to the west and Dahong Mountain to the east. In the ancient times, it was called "eight hundred *Li* (Chinese unit of length) of Wudang" because of its grand scale. It was praised as the "No. 1 Mountain in the World" by Mi Fei, a master of calligraphy and Chinese paintings in the Northern Song Dynasty (960-1279) for its scenery as magnificent as Mount Tai's, as unique as

自古以来，武当山就以超凡脱俗的自然风光吸引着崇尚自然的道家来此修炼讲道。这里道教建筑规模宏伟，星罗棋布。据统计，唐至清代共建庙宇500多处，庙房2万余间。明代达到鼎盛，永乐皇帝朱棣在1412年起先后动用30万民工，历时12年之久，在武当山大兴土木，营建了从山麓到金顶长达70公里的

Mount Huang's and as tranquil as Mount Yandang's. Mount Wudang's gorgeous and mysterious scenery includes upper and down eighteen tortuous winding pathways around the central Heavenly Pillar Summit (*Tianzhu Feng*), seventy-two mountain peaks and the scenic site of "overlapping shadows of golden halls". The Heavenly Pillar Summit, the main summit in Mount Wudang, is 1,612 meters above sea level, known as "one pillar upholding the sky". It is surrounded by the Southern Rock Peak (*Nanyan Feng*), Double Pen Peak(*Shuangbi Feng*), Jade Goddness Peak (*Yunu*

● 武当山风光
Scenery of Mount Wudang

"神道"，并建成33座大型建筑群，殿宇2万多间，建筑面积达160万平方米，还修成了39座桥梁，12座亭台。现在，武当山依然完好保存着129处道观殿宇、牌坊亭阁，还有珍贵文物7400多件，被誉为"道教文物宝库"。

• 武当山风光
Scenery of Mount Wudang

Feng), Lover Watching Peak (*Wanglang Feng*), Immortal Peak (*Xianren Feng*) all leaning towards the center forming a scenic wonder of ten thousand mountains coming together.

Since ancient times Mount Wudang's natural beauty that transcends the mortal world attracted many Taoist masters who admire nature to practice and preach Taoism here. Embellished with magnificent Taoist building structures, it is estimated that Mount Wudang had seen over 500 temples and 20,000 subsidiary rooms built from the Tang Dynasty to the Qing Dynasty. It reached its peak in the Ming Dynasty. Emperor Zhudi of the Ming Dynasty deployed 300,000 workers to build a "spirit way" (*Shendao*) of 70 kilometers long in 12 years. During this period, 33 building complexes and over 20,000 halls covering a construction area of 160,000 square meters were built. Moreover, an additional 39 bridges and 12 pavilions were built. Currently there are still 129 sites of well-preserved temples, towers, memorial gates and pagodas which house over 7,400 valuable cultural relics. Mount Wudang is considered the treasure house of Taoist cultural relics.

紫霄宫

紫霄宫位于武当山主峰天柱峰东北的展旗峰下，建于明永乐十一年（1413年），是武当山现存宫观中规模最大、保存最完整的一座。紫霄宫殿宇共分四进，自上而下依次为龙虎殿、十方堂、紫霄殿和父母殿，两侧以配房等建筑分割为三进院落。龙虎殿内供奉青龙、白虎

- 武当山紫霄殿
  Purple Heaven Palace (*Zixiao Dian*) in Mount Wudang

Purple Heaven Palace (*Zixiao Gong*)

Purple Heaven Palace (*Zixiao Gong*) is located below the Zhangqi Peak northeast of the main Heavenly Pillar Peak of Mount Wudang. Built in 1413 during the Ming Dynasty, it is the largest and best preserved extant temple in Mount Wudang. It is divided into four levels with the Dragon and Tiger Hall (*Longhu Dian*) at the upper level, Four Directions Hall (*Shifang Diang*), Purple Heaven Hall (*Zixiao Dian*) and Parents Hall (*Fumu Dian*) at the lower level, each in a three-layer courtyard built with supplemental rooms on the left and right wings. The Dragon and Tiger Hall enshrines clay

泥塑神将。十方堂内供奉铜铸镏金真武像。紫霄殿为紫霄宫的正殿，殿内神龛中供奉着明代御制铜铸镏金真武神像，为真武老、中、青年龄段和文、武装束的塑像，殿的左右两厢还供奉着28尊不同规格的真武神像。父母殿内供奉着真武大帝的父母，即净乐国王明真大帝和善胜皇后，两边神龛分别供奉着观音菩萨和三霄娘娘。规模宏大的道教建筑群、幽深静雅的自然环境使得紫霄宫被视为"紫霄福地"。

金殿

金殿位于天柱峰顶峰，以在阳光下灼灼生辉而得名。金殿始建于明代，为铜铸仿木结构宫殿式建筑，面积约160平方米。殿面宽与进深均为三间，阔4.4米，深3.15米，高5.54米，四周12根立柱。金殿及殿内神像、香案、供器均为铜铸，是在北京铸造好后运到武当山的，总重量约90吨，是中国现存元、明、清几座铸铜殿堂中最华丽、制作技艺最精湛的一座，具有极高的科学和艺术价值。殿内正中宝座上供奉着真武大帝铜铸镏金像，神案下有

statues of two deity warriors: the azure dragon and the white tiger. The Four Directions Hall houses a golden bronze statue of the Great Emperor Zhenwu, a famous immortal in Taoism. The Purple Heaven Hall is the main hall of the Purple Heaven Palace, it enshrines in the alcove of golden bronze statue of the Great Emperor Zhenwu in different ages and in civilian and military outfits, which were made by the court of the Ming Dynasty. On both sides of the hall stand another 28 statues of the Great Emperor Zhenwu in different sizes. The Parents Hall (*Fumu Dian*) houses the Great Emperor Zhenwu's parents, Emperor Mingzhen and Empress Shansheng with the shrines of Bodhisattva Guanyin and three female immortals in the side alcoves. The integration of magnificent Taoist building complexes with the unfathomable, tranquil natural environment won the Purple Heaven Palace the fame of "the Blessed Land of Purple Heaven".

Gold Hall (*Jin Dian*)

The Gold Hall (*Jin Dian*) at the top of the Heavenly Pillar Peak got its name for its shining radiance under the sun. The hall, built in the Ming Dynasty based

● 武当山金殿（图片提供：全景正片）
Mount Wudang Gold Hall

龟蛇二将。整座建筑结构严谨，合缝精密，虽经五百多年的严寒酷暑，至今仍辉煌如初，显示了中国铸造工艺发展的高度和水平，堪称现存古建筑和铸造工艺中的一颗璀璨明珠。

on the imperial palace style of wooden structures, covers an area of 160 square meters supported by 12 columns in three sections of 4.4 meters wide, 3.15 meters deep and 5.54 meters high each. The structure itself and the statues, incense tables and utilities were all cast in bronze in Beijing and then transported to Mount Wudang. Total weight of them is 90 tons. It is the most splendid and most exquisitely crafted of all existing bronze halls in China built in the Yuan, Ming and Qing dynasties. It has very high scientific and artistic values. In the center of the palace enshrines the gold statue of the Great Emperor Zhenwu. Under the incense table, there are another two celestial warriors of turtle and snake. The whole building is structured with seamless precision. After five hundred years of bitter cold or torried heat, it still shines as brilliantly as before demonstrating China's highly developed bronze casting techniques and an image of a bright star in the extant ancient building structures.

武当拳

　　武当拳发源于道教圣地武当山，俗称"内家拳"，是中国武术一大名宗。武当拳的创始人是北宋时武当山著名道士张三丰，他创造的拳术称为动静结合的太极拳。武当武术以"道"为指导，处处闪耀着道家的智慧。张三丰曾说过："欲令天下豪杰延年益寿，不图技击之末学。"这充分体现了道家与世无争的特征，也说明武当武术为的不是"打架"，而是以养生为主旨，欲令天下习武之人能延年益寿。

Wudang-Style Martial Art (*Wudang Quan*)

Wudang-style martial art started in the Taoist sacred site of Mount Wudan, commonly known as "internal school of boxing", a notable school of Chinese martial arts. The founder of the Wudang-style martial art Zhang Sanfeng, a famous Taoist monk in Mount Wudang during the Northern Song Dynasty, invented Tai Chi Chuan, a style combining both quick and slow martial art movements. The core of the Wudang-style martial art takes the Taoism as the guidance. Every technique shows the Taoist wisdom. Zhang Sanfeng once said that practicing martial arts was not for the techniques, but for better health and longevity of every martial art master. His thinking fully demonstrates the characteristics of Taoism of avoiding confrontations and the belief that Wudang martial art is not for violence, but for keeping good health and a long life.

• 太极拳
Tai chi Chuan

> 青城山

青城山位于四川省都江堰市西南、成都平原西北部，景区面积200平方公里。相传黄帝曾经封青城山为五岳丈人，因此青城山古称"丈人山"。后由于山上林木葱郁，四季常青，整座山巍峨壮观如同一座城郭，故有"青城"的美称。青城山景色优美，自古就有"青城天下幽"的美誉。山中林幽水秀，云霞缥缈，溪泉逶迤，构成了一幅仙境胜景，有三十六峰、八大洞、七十二小洞、一百零八景之说。

青城山是道教的发祥地之一。早在东汉时期，就有张道陵天师在青城山赤城崖舍创立道教并积极传教，在唐朝时期进入最为鼎盛的时期。山中道观多达四十多处，至今依然道脉繁衍，

> Mount Qingcheng (*Qingcheng Shan*)

Mount Qingcheng (*Qingcheng Shan*) sits in the southwest of Dujiangyan City, Sichuan Province and to the northwest of Chengdu plains with a scenic area of 200 square kilometers. According to legend the Emperor Huang named Mount Qingcheng "Father of Five Sacred Mountains", hence the name "Mount Father" in ancient times. The name Mount Qingcheng (literally "Mount Green City") came from its evergreen dense forests and magnificent mountain range that looks like a city. It has the fame of "Qingcheng is the most serene place in the world" since ancient times. Its scenic fairyland beauty of deep forests, clear water and misty clouds consists of thirty-six peaks, eight caverns, seventy-two small caves and one hundred and eight scenic sites.

• 青城山风光
Scenery of Mount Qingcheng

千年不衰。青城山在道教中依然有着崇高的地位和巨大的影响力。青城山的宫观，清代重修后，至今基本保存完好，主要有建福宫、常道观、祖师殿、上清宫、老君阁等。宫观建筑崇尚自然，朴素大气，与山峦、溪谷和谐共存，融为一体，如同一幅天然图画。

建福宫

建福宫坐落于青城山的丈人峰下，始建于晋代，原址在青城天国山中，唐开元十八年（730年）迁于今址，南宋诗人范成大曾在此为宋帝祈祷，故皇帝特赐名"会庆建

Mount Qingcheng is one of the birthplaces of Taoism. As early as in the Eastern Han Dynasty (25-220), Master Zhang Daoling came here to establish, practice and preach Taoism. Taoism became most popular during the Tang Dynasty (618-907) when over forty Taoist temples were built in Mount Qingcheng. Today it still has a very lofty position and great influence in Chinese Taoism after thousands of years. The building structures in Mount Qingcheng were repaired in Qing Dynasty and have been well preserved till the present day. The main extant buildings include the Temple of Established Happiness (*Jianfu Gong*), Temple of Taoist Rules

• 青城山建福宫
Palace of Established Happiness (*Jianfu Gong*) in Mount Qingcheng

福宫"，沿用至今。建福宫现存建筑为清代光绪年间重建，主要由大殿、缘云阁、水心亭等建筑组成。三重大殿分别供奉五岳丈人、太上老君、东华帝君等神像。其中殿内柱上的394字的对联被赞为"青城一绝"。气派非凡的道教建筑前有清溪、后有乳泉相拥，宫内壁画、楹联弥足珍贵。

老君阁

老君阁位于青城山海拔1600多米高的第一峰的彭祖峰顶上。老君阁阁基共六层，下方上圆，外观呈塔形。老君阁造像以中国现代著

(*Changdao Guan*), Hall of the Ancestral Master (*Zushi Dian*), Temple of Highest Clarity (*Shangqing Gong*) and Lord Laozi Tower (*Laojun Ge*). These ancient Taoist structures are simple and full of natural qualities that make them immerse with the mountain ridges, valleys and water harmoniously creating a beautiful painting of nature.

Palace of Established Happiness (*Jianfu Gong*)

Palace of Established Happiness (*Jianfu Gong*) sits below the Father Peak (*Zhangren Feng*) of Mount Qingcheng. It was built in the Jin Dynasty and was moved from its original site in *Tianguo*

名画家徐悲鸿当年在青城山的遗作《紫气东来》为蓝本，由青城山道友绘制、塑造而成。老君像高13.6米，连牛身通高16米。登高望远，青城诸峰景色可尽收眼底，夜晚还可以赏神灯、观日出、看云海，风光无限。

Peak to its current site in the year of 730 during the Tang Dynasty. Fan Chengda, a poet of the Southern Song Dynasty once prayed for the Song emperor here. Therefore the Emperor bestowed the name "Temple of Celebrated and Established Happiness", which has been used till the present day. The extant structure was renovated around 1888 during the Qing Dynasty including the main hall, *Yuanyun* Pavilion and *Shuixin* Pavilion, which house the shrines respectively the Father of Five Mountains (*Wuyue Zhangren*), Lord Laozi and Taoist Emperor Donghua (*Donghua Dijun*). The couplets of 394 words carved on the pillars in the main hall were acclaimed "a wonder in Mount Qingcheng". This elegant Taoist structure is of great cultural and artistic value with wall paintings and couplets as well as streams flowing in the front and spring fountains in the back.

Lord Laozi Tower (*Laojun Ge*)

Lord Laozi Tower is located on Pengzu Peak (*Pengzu Feng*), the No. 1 peak

• 青城山老君阁 (图片提供：FOTOE)
Lord Laozi Tower (*Laojun Ge*) in Mount Qingcheng

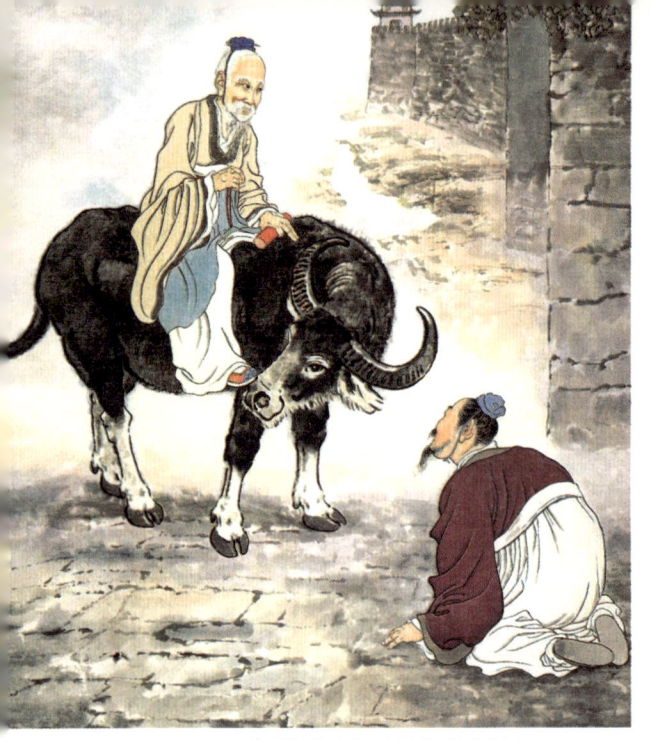

• 《紫气东来》（现代 徐悲鸿）
Purple Cloud from the East by Xu Beihong, Modern

圆明宫

　　圆明宫坐落在青城山的北木鱼山上，始建于明代万历年间，因供奉圆明道母天尊而得名。宫内有四重殿堂：前为灵祖殿，供奉道教护法神王灵官神像；二殿为老君殿，供奉太上老君；三殿为斗姆殿，斗姆即圆明道母天尊，为北斗众星之母；后殿为三官殿，供奉天、地、水三官大帝及全真道（道教的一支流派）的吕祖、邱祖和重阳祖师。

in Mount Qingcheng at 1,600 meters above sea level. The pavilion is a six-story building of a pagoda shape sitting on a square platform with a round top. The sculptures of Laozi and his cow were painted and made by Mount Qingcheng Taoist believers based on the painting *Purple Cloud from the East* by the famous Chinese modern artist Xu Beihong. The statue of Laozi is 13.6 meters high and has a total height of 16 meters including the cow. Standing on top of the pavilion the entire Mount Qingcheng unfolds before visitors' eyes. It is the place to enjoy divine lights at night, sunrise in the morning and sea of clouds of infinite scenery.

Yuanming Palace

Built between 1573 and 1620 during the Ming Dynasty, *Yuanming* Palace stands on the Wooden Fish Mountain (*Muyu Shan*) north of Mount Qingcheng. It was named after Taoist Empress of Yuanming. The palace has four halls: Hall of Spiritual Ancestor (*Lingzu Dian*) enshrining the Taoist God Wang Lingguan, Hall of Lord Laozi (*Laojun Dian*) enshrining the Lord Laozi, Hall of Tao Empress of Yuanming (*Doumu Dian*) and Hall of Three Great Emperor

三清殿

三清殿是常道观的主殿，殿前铺设通廊石阶九级，前檐排列大石圆柱六根，立在高1.2米雕工精致的石狮、麒麟和独角兽柱础上。殿堂横列五间，重檐飞瓦，古朴宏伟。其正中高悬清康熙皇帝御书"丹台

- 《青城山途中图》（现代 黄宾虹）
On Way to Mount Qingcheng by Huang Binhong, Modern

of Elements who are in charge of heaven, earth and water, and Master Lv, Master Qiu and Master Chongyang, who are founders of Quanzhen Taoist School.

Hall of Three Purities (*Sanqing Dian*)

Hall of Three Purities (*Sanqing Dian*) is the main hall in the Temple of Taoist Rules. In front of the hall there are a passageway of nine stone steps, six round stone pillars in a row and exquisitely carved 1.2-meter high stone animals of a lion, a kylin and a unicorn at the pillar base. There are five rooms with a horizontal tablet of "Red Platform in Green Cave" inscribed by Emperor Kangxi of the Qing Dynasty hanging from the high ceiling. In the hall there are three highest gods of Tao: God of Jade Purity—the Universal Lord of Primordial Beginning (*Yuqing Yuanshi Tianzun*), God of Supreme Purity—the Universal Lord of Numinous Treasure (*Shangqing Lingbao Tianzun*) and God of Grand Purity—the Universal Lord of the Way and its Virtue (*Taiqing Daode Tianzun*). The top floor is Hall of the Boundless (*Wuji Dian*) decorated with eight wooden screen decorations of colorful and lively hollow carved hibiscus flowers, lotus

青城山三清殿 (图片提供: FOTOE)
Hall of Three Purities (*Sanqing Dian*) in Mount Qingcheng

碧洞"匾额。殿内供奉道教最高神"三清",即玉清元始天尊、上清灵宝天尊和太清道德天尊。楼上是无极殿,有明代的木雕屏花八扇,全系镂空雕刻的芙蓉、荷花、孔雀等,形象生动,色彩明快。三清殿供奉的是三清尊神,中间是玉清元始天尊,他手持元珠象征洪元世纪;右边是上清灵宝天尊,他怀抱如意,象征混元世纪;左边是太清道德天尊,也就是老子,他手持宝

flowers and peacocks. Standing in the middle of the hall is God of Jade Purity, who holds a Pearl of Creation, signifying his role in creating the Universe from void and chaos (*Hongyuan Shiji*). To his right is the God of Supreme Purity with a wishful *Ruyi* instrument representing the second phase of Creation where the *Yang* was separated from the *Yin* (*Hunyuan Shji*). To his left is the God of Grand Purity, a reincarnation of Laozi symbolizing the completion of Creation,

扇象征太初世纪，张道陵创教时把他尊为教祖。三清是道教的最高境界，这三位天尊也是道教信奉的三位最高尊神，三清殿也是由此得名。

and the act of fanning represents the spreading of Tao to all Mankind (*Taichu Shiji*). When Zhang Daoling founded Taoism he regarded Laozi the Taoist Saint. These Taoist gods are the highest Gods worshipped by Taoism believers and this hall was named after them.

洪元世纪、混元世纪、太初世纪

中国的道教将宇宙诞生至今的历史分为三个阶段，即洪元世纪、混元世纪和太初世纪。洪元世纪指的是最初天地未分的阶段，其后盘古开天辟地，身化万物，宇宙始生，而盘古的一缕精气最终化为元始天尊。混元世纪指的是从宇宙始生至原始社会的阶段，当时的世界常常火山爆发，地震频生，于是天地间又孕育了另一位大神，即灵宝天尊，解救生灵。太初世纪指的是原始社会至今，当时修行风气鼎盛，诞生了无数神通广大的传奇人物。

Hongyuan, Hunyuan and Taichu Centuries

Taoism in China divides the history of universe into three periods: *Hongyuan*, *Hunyuan* and *Taichu* Centuries. *Hongyuan* represents the time of pre-Creation when Pangu separated the one universe into earth and sky, turned his body parts into everything in the cosmos and eventually his spirit became the Universal Lord of the Primordial Beginning. *Hunyuan* represents growing period from the beginning of the universe to the primitive society where volcanoes erupted and earthquakes occurred frequently, thus giving birth to another Taoist god, the Universal Lord of the Numinous Treasure to save creatures. *Taichu* represents the development from the primitive society to present. The popularity of Taoism at the time generated numerous legends about these heroes of supernatural powers.

> 齐云山

　　齐云山古称"白岳",位于安徽黄山市休宁县境内,因其"一石插天,与云并齐",故名"齐云山"。齐云山风景区面积为110平方公里,海拔高度585米,是一处以道

● 齐云山风光 (图片提供:全景正片)
Scenery of Mount Qiyun

> Mount Qiyun (*Qiyun Shan*)

Mount Qiyun (*Qiyun Shan*), ancient name White Mountain (*Bai Yue*) is situated in Xiuning County in Huangshan City, Anhui Province. It was named after the ancient saying "one stone shooting up to the sky, as high as the cloud",

教文化和丹霞地貌为特色的山岳风景名胜区，与黄山、九华山并称为中国皖南三大名山。齐云山属丹霞地貌，峰峦怪谲，怪石嶙岣，赤如丹砂，灿若红霞。其中的香炉峰、五老峰、三姑峰神奇灵幻，石桥岩、紫宵岩巧夺天工，山洞幽幻莫测、恬淡静逸，珠帘泉、飞雨泉飞珠溅玉，灵气逼人。

齐云山道教始于唐乾元年间，有道人龚栖霞曾在栖真岩辟谷修道，后繁盛于明清。齐云山以玉虚宫、真武殿和玄天素宫、天清殿、洞天福地等最为有名。山中的石门寺始建于唐元和四年（809年），寺庙建筑宏伟壮观，寺内历代雕刻佛像、道家绘画不胜枚举。而令人心旷神怡的湖光山色和历史悠久的道教文化令无数文人流连忘返。李白、朱熹、徐霞客等都先后登临，并留下了众多的摩崖石刻和名碑墨宝。现在，齐云山尚存摩崖石刻305处、碑刻232块、古石坊刻7座。这些石刻或雄劲豪放，或清婉秀丽，具有极高的艺术价值，不管是质量还是数量都堪称"江南第一"。

hence Mount Qiyun meaning a mountain as high as the clouds. The scenic area of Mount Qiyun covers 110 square kilometers at an altitude of 585 meters. It is well-known for its Buddhist culture and *Danxia* landforms, and joined by Mount Huang and Mount Jiuhua as the Three Famous Mountains in Southern Anhui province. Mount Qiyun's *Danxia* geomorphologic landscape features soaring peaks and grotesque rocks as red as cinnabar and the sunset glow. These scenic sites include the mystic peaks of Incense Burner Peak (*Xianglu Feng*), Five Immortals Peak (*Wulao Feng*) and Three Celestial Nuns Peak (*Sangu Feng*), marvelously shaped Stone Bridge Cliff (*Shiqiao Yan*) and Purple Night Cliff (*Zixiao Yan*), unfathomable and silent caverns, and splashing Pearl Curtain Spring (*Zhulian Quan*) and Flying Rain Spring (*Feiyu Quan*).

Taoist activities in Mount Qiyun started between the year of 758 and 760 during the Tang Dynasty when Gong Xixia, a Taoist monk, came to practice self-cultivation on fasting. After that, Taoism became popular in Mount Qiyun during the Ming and Qing dynasties. The most famous Taoist structures in Mount Qiyun are the Imperial Void

玉虚宫

玉虚宫位于齐云山的紫霄崖下,是道教宫观。玉虚宫始建于明代正德十年(1515年),建筑依山而建,气势恢宏,工艺精巧。宫前由"太乙真庆宫""五虚阙""治世仁威宫"三个石坊组成,坊高17

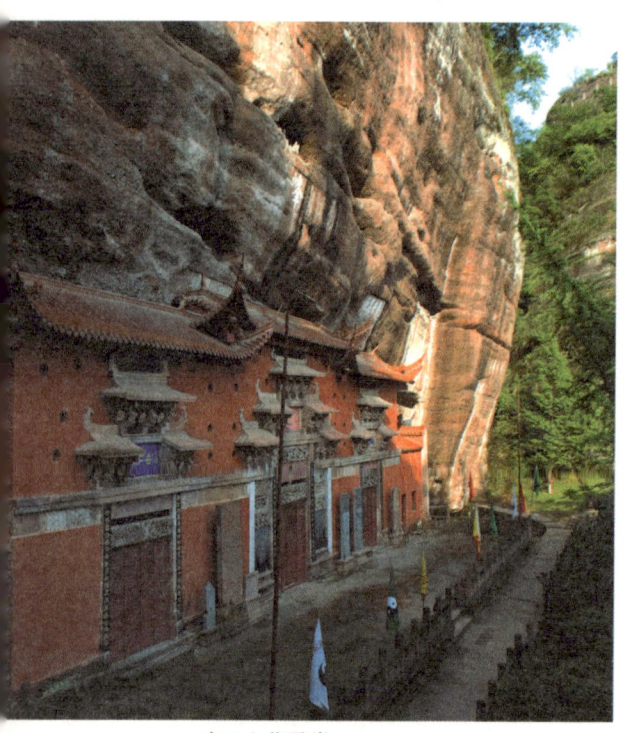

● 齐云山紫霄崖 (图片提供:全景正月)
紫霄崖是齐云山丹霞地貌中最为壮观的地质景观之一,长200余米,高150余米。

Purple Night Cliff (Zixiao Ya) in Mount Qiyun
The Purple Night Cliff, 200 meters long and 150 meters high, is the most magnificent Danxia geomorphologic landform in Mount Qiyun.

Palace (*Yuxu Gong*), Hall of the Great Emperor Zhenwu (*Zhenwu Dian*), North Heaven White Palace (*Xuantian Sugong*), Clear Heaven Hall (*Tianqing Dian*), and Earthly Heaven Cave and Blessed Land (*Dongtian Fudi*). The Stone Gate Temple (*Shimen Si*) of Mount Qiyun was built in the year of 809 during the Tang Dynasty. This magnificent building houses many Buddha sculptures and Taoist paintings of different dynasties. Mount Qiyun's enthralling landscape and a long history of Taoist culture attracted innumerable Chinese literati such as Li Bai, Zhu Xi and Xu Xiake to climb up to the mountain leaving behind a large number of cliff-side carvings and stone tablets of their famous calligraphy and inscriptions. At present Mount Qiyun has existing 305 cliff-side carvings, 232 stone tablets and 7 ancient engraved tablets, of which some have a bold and powerful style and some are pretty and elegant. All of them have extremely high artistic value. They are considered "No. 1 art works in regions south of the Yangtze River (*Jiangnan*)" in both quantities and qualities.

Imperial Void Palace (*Yuxu Gong*)

The Imperial Void Palace below the Purple Night Cliff is a Taoist temple

米，以红色砂岩镌成，周围饰以神鸟异兽图案的浮雕，整个造型古朴典雅，独具特色。宫内便是石洞，洞内主祀真武大帝。

洞天福地

洞天福地是齐云山摩崖石刻和碑铭集中的地区，其中最为出

constructed by the mountain side in the year of 1515 during the Ming Dynasty. In front of the magnificent temple there are three stone gateways of Palace of Primordial Beginning Lord (*Taiyi Zhenqing Gong*), Five Void Gateway (*Wuxu Que*) and Palace of Ruling the World with Benevolence and Power (*Zhishi Renwei Gong*). These three classically and uniquely shaped gateways are 17-meter high, built with red sandstone and embossment of divine birds and supernatural beasts. The whole

● 齐云山寿字崖 (图片提供：FOTOE)
Mount Qiyun Cliff of Longevity Character (*Shouzi Ya*)

名的是栖真岩、忠烈岩、寿字崖三处。据传，栖真岩是齐云山最早的道士——唐朝的栖霞真人修行的地方；忠烈岩是祭祀关公的地方；而寿字崖的"寿"字是清代慈禧太后的手笔，这个巨大的"寿"字，直径达到230厘米。走过寿字崖，便见一个宽敞的石洞，游人可以通过，纯属天工所造，为"崖下窟窿"，称之为一天门，这里的摩崖石刻和碑铭数目很多，琳琅满目，为"白岳碑林"。

stone gateway is simple and elegant, with unique characteristics. Inside is the cavern which houses and worships the statue of the Great Emperor Zhenwu.

Earthly Heaven Cave and Blessed Land (*Dongtian Fudi*)

Earthly Heaven Cave and Blessed Land is an area with the highest concentration of clif-fside carvings and rock inscriptions in Mount Qiyun. The most famous ones are *Qizhen* Cliff, Valiant Cliff (*Zhonglie Yan*) and Cliff of Longevity Character (*Shouzi Ya*). *Qizhen* Cliff was where the earliest Taoist monk Qizhen of the Tang Dynasty practiced self-cultivation; the Valiant Cliff is the place to pay homage to Lord Guan; and the huge Chinese character carved on the Cliff of Longevity Character is a copy of the Qing Dynasty Empress Dowager Cixi's handwriting, which is 230 centimeters in diameter. Walking past this cliff, the visitor will see a cavern that wide enough to go through. It is a natural cavern just below the cliff known as the "hole under the cliff, and "one gateway to the sky" (*Yitian Men*). The dazzling array of rock inscriptions inside is called "stone tablet forests of the white mountain".

关公

　　关公，名关羽，是三国时期（220—280）的著名将领，自蜀汉开国皇帝刘备于乡里聚众起兵开始，便一直追随，是刘备最为信任的将领之一。关羽以忠贞、守义、勇猛和武艺高强著称于世，他去世后，其忠勇的形象逐渐被后人神化，一直是民间祭祀的对象，被尊称为"关公"。

Lord Guan

Lord Guan or Guan Yu was a famous general in the Three Kingdoms Period (220-280). He had served under Liu Bei since Liu's uprising in his hometown till Liu became the first emperor of the State of Shu-Han. He was the general most trusted by Liu Bei. Guan was respected for his loyalty, righteousness, braveness and prowess. After his death, Guan was gradually deified in folklore and became Lord Guan worshipped by people.

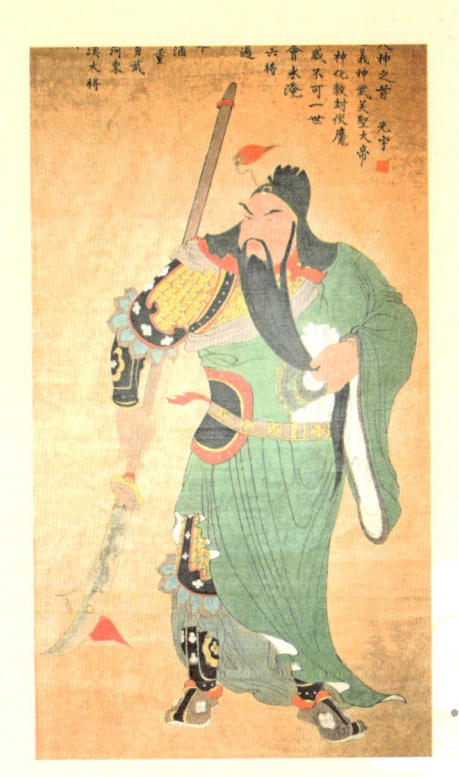

• 关公像
Portrait of Lord Guan

真仙洞府

真仙洞府位于数百丈高的黑虎崖悬崖底部，由八仙洞、圆通洞、罗汉洞、雨君洞、文昌洞、老君洞、珠帘洞、玉虚宫等组成，是以前道士修炼居住的地方。真仙洞府内供奉着各路神仙塑像，既有道

齐云山真仙洞府 (图片提供：全景正片)
Immortal Cavern in Mount Qiyun (*Zhenxian Dongfu*)

Immortal Cavern (*Zhenxian Dongfu*)

The Immortal Cavern (*Zhenxian Dongfu*) at the bottom of the towering Black Tiger Cliff (*Heihu Ya*) consists of the Eight Immortals Cave (*Baxian Dong*), Imperial Fund Cave (*Yuantong Dong*), Arhat Cave (*Luohan Dong*), Rain God Cave (*Yujun Dong*), Cave of God of Literature (*Wenchang Dong*), Lord Laozi Cave (*Laojun Dong*), Pearl Curtain Cave (*Zhulian Dong*) and Jade Piety Palace (*Yuqian Gong*). It was a dwelling place for Taoist monks to practice self-cultivation. The Immortal Cavern enshrines different schools of immortals, both Buddhist and Taoist. Confucious, Taoist and Buddhist cultures are merged together inside the carven, which became one of the best sceneries in Mount Qiyun, On the precipices of the cavern carved hundreds of ancient rock inscriptions which laid out in an orderly fashion forming a long stele corridor. The most striking are the four huge characters on the sheer cliff: *Kai Tian Shen Xiu* meaning the magic beauty under sky. These four characters have become a visible sign for the Immortal Cavern. The unique geographical location of the Immortal Cavern creates a unique scenic

教的神仙也有佛教的菩萨佛像，是儒、道、佛三家文化融合的地方，这种特色使其成为齐云山的精粹之一。真仙洞府崖壁上有数以百计的古代碑碣、摩崖石刻。它们依次排列，形成碑道长廊，其中最为醒目的是崖壁上的"天开神秀"四个大字,气势不凡,为真仙洞府的显著标志。真仙洞府独特的地理位置也造就了它独特的迷人风景，无论晴雨，崖顶总有泉珠散落，形成薄薄水帘，世人称"珍珠帘"。下有碧莲池塘，池水晶莹清碧，景色清幽，与香炉峰遥遥相望。

太素宫

太素宫是齐云山的主要道观之一，原名"佑圣真武祠"，始建于南宋宝庆年间。明世宗嘉靖十一年（1532年），龙虎山正一派第四十八代天师张彦頨奏令道众赴齐云山为皇帝建醮祈嗣，果获应验。于是皇帝敕令扩建真武祠，改名为"玄天太素宫"。太素宫坐南朝北，占地面积1600余平方米，由"玄天金阙"石坊、宫门、前殿、正殿、后殿、客堂、斋堂、道舍等

beauty. Whether rain or shine, there are always splashing drops of water scattering over the top of the cliff, forming a very thin curtain known as the "pearl curtain", below which is the green lotus pond (*Bilian Chitang*). All of them create a scene of clear spring water in tranquility echoing with the Incense Burner Peak in the distance.

Supreme White Palace (*Taisu Gong*)

The Supreme White Palace is one of the main Taoist temples in Mount Qiyun, the original name being "Blessed Sacred Zhenwu Temple" (*Yousheng Zhenwu Ci*). It was built between the year of 1225 and 1227 during the Southern Song Dynasty. In the year of 1532 Tao Master Zhang Yanyu of the forty-eighth generation of Mount Longhu Taoist School proposed to heaven to have Taoist disciples build a temple on Mount Qiyun, and it became effective afterwards. So the emperor ordered to expand the temple and changed its name from Zhenwu Temple to North Heaven Supreme White Palace (*Xuantian Taisu Gong*) taking Supreme White Palace for short. The north-facing palace covers an area of 1,600 square meters comprising the North Heaven Golden Gateway, the palace entrance, the front hall, the main hall, the

建筑组成。该宫周围形成一条街道，即月华街。月华街是道士与山上居民杂居之所，也是山上的街市，同时又是香客、游人住宿之地。月华街现有古道房8座，还有许多徽派民居，它们与宫观、院房组成一个密集的建筑群。

back hall, guest rooms, Hall of Abstinence and living quarters. Surrounding the palace is the Yuehua Street, a place where both Taoist monks and ordinary people live together. It is the street market in Mount Qiyun and accommodations for both Taoist pilgrims and tourists. The town is densely populated with eight ancient Taoist structures and many Hui style dwellings for local residents. Together with Supereme white Palace and other rooms, they consists a cluster of buildings.

- 齐云山太素宫 (图片提供：FOTOE)
  Supreme White Palace (*Taisu Gong*) in Mount Qiyun

百鸟衔泥塑玄帝

相传齐云山玄武太素真人朝夕讲经说法,潜心修炼,道成后,被称为"北方真武大帝",镇定北方,掌管人间一切善恶,普济众生。

一日,玄武太素真人出山云游四海,遍访名山,后来被齐云山的秀美风光吸引,决心在这里修建行宫,招徕香火。就在此时,忽见一朵祥云飘临,化作白鹤仙子,拱揖参拜。玄武谢过,将方才所思告知白鹤仙子,白鹤仙子应命告别玄帝,立即传召全山百鸟,即日兴工。自此,百鸟云集,羽翼蔽日,众志成城。不几日,塑起一尊玄帝偶像,威严夺目。

光阴荏苒,到了南宋宝庆年间,有个云游道士自黟北来齐云山,梦见一道长披发跣足,对他说:"吾居齐云岩,已候驾多时。"梦醒寻至齐云岩,见一泥像与梦中无异,又惊又喜,遂动员在山居士募捐装饰金身,创立了"佑圣真武祠",燃起香火,日夜供奉。后来,只要四乡遇有蝗灾、旱涝,或祈福求嗣者均有求必应,神威江南。道士也纷纷驻守山上,在岩洞内、道房供上玄武帝像,香火日趋兴盛,成为一处久负盛名的道教圣地。

Hundred Birds Clay Sculpture of the Great Emperor of Zhenwu

It is said that the North Immortal of Taisu taught sutras day and night while practicing

• 《齐云山图》(现代 黄宾虹)
Painting of Mount Qiyun by Huang Binghong, Modern

self-cultivations. When he completed his practice, he became the North Emperor of Zhenwu in charge of the North regions and controlling the good and the evil in the afterworld of salvation.

One day he went on an cruise around the earth visiting famous mountains. Fascinated by the beautiful scenery of Mount Qiyun, he was determined to build a temple here to attract pilgrims. Right at this moment, a cloud passed by and turned into a white crane fairy. Zhenwu expressed gratitude for her action and told her about his idea, who immediately called on hundreds of birds in the mountain to start the construction. In a few days, hundreds of birds flew over with mud held in their mouths and built a solemn statue of Emperor Zhenwu.

As time went by, another Taoist priests came to Mount Qiyun from Yibei (Yixian County, Anhui Province) and dreamed a Taoist priest with long hair and bare feet, who said to him, "I have been living in Mount Qiyun waiting for you for a long time." When he woke up from the dream, the Taoist priest saw a clay statue looking exactly the same as the one in his dream. Surprised and excited, he encouraged people living in the mountain to donate money for a gilded statue. The Blessed Sacred Zhewu Temple was founded then with incense burning day and night for pilgrims. Later when there was drought, flood or plague of locusts, the statue granted watever was requested by its believers. As a result its divine power became well-known throughout south of Yangtze. Taoist monks came to dwell on the mountain in crowds. Inside the cavern they enshrined the statue of the Emperor Zhenwu with increasingly popular incense burning rituals, eventually making the temple a permanent Taoist sacred site.

> 龙虎山

　　龙虎山位于江西省鹰潭市郊西南16公里处，原名"云锦山"。东汉中叶，道教创始人张道陵遍访名山大川，最后选择了龙虎山肇基炼丹，"丹成而龙虎现，山因得

• 龙虎山风光 (图片提供：全景正片)
Scenery of Mount Longhu

> Mount Longhu (*Longhu Shan*)

Mount Longhu (*Longhu Shan*, literally Mount Dragon and Tiger) is located in the suburbs 16 kilometers southwest of Yintan City, Jiangxi Province. Originally it was called Mount Yunjin (literally Mount Cloud Brocade). In the middle period of the Eastern Han Dynasty, Zhang Daoling, founder of Taoism visited famous mountains and rivers in China and finally chose Mount Longhu to be the place for him to make elixir

名"。龙虎山因而也成为中国道教的发祥地之一。龙虎山景区面积达200平方公里，主要分布于泸溪河（又名"上清河"）两岸，风景十分秀丽。独特的丹霞地貌成就了龙虎山雄、奇、险、秀、幽的宜人风光。奇山怪石、茂林修竹在清澈的泸溪河两岸随着水流逶迤而下，构成了"一条涧水琉璃合，万叠云山紫翠堆"的奇丽景象，水中有景，景中有水，绚烂多彩的碧水丹崖令游客流连忘返、沉醉其中。

龙虎山自古以"神仙都所""人间福地"而闻名天下，龙虎山神奇灵秀的丹山碧水，远离尘嚣，是修炼的理想之地。虽然当年道教建造的宫、观、院多已不存，但规模宏大的上清宫部分建筑和历代天师起居之所的"嗣汉天师府"至今尚存。

天师府

天师府是历代天师生活起居之所和祀神之处，原称"真仙观"，建在龙虎山脚下。天师府南向琵琶峰，门临泸溪河，北靠西华山，依山傍水，气势非凡。经过历年修葺

of immortality. The legend said that a dragon and a tiger appeared when the elixir was produced, hence the name Mount Longhu (Dragon and Tiger) and one of the birthplaces of Chinese Taoism. Mount Longhu's scenic area covers more than 200 square kilometers along both sides of Luxi River (also known as Shangqing River). The distinct Danxia geomorphologic landform demonstrates the magnificence, precipitousness, uniqueness, serenity and elegance of Mount Longhu's scenic beauty, which is described in a poem as a stream of colorful water flowing through layers of clouds and green mountain ridges. The strangely shaped mountain cliffs and rocks among lush green trees and bamboos undulate continuously along the Luxi River creating the scenery of "view in the water and view with the water" making Mount Longhu an unforgettable place for tourists.

Since the ancient times, Mount Longhu has always enjoyed the reputation of "a celestial residence" or "a paradise on earth". The beautiful scenery of mysterious, spiritual mountain with clear water makes Mount Longhu a perfect place for Taoists to practice self-cultivation. Most of the temples built

龙虎山天师府玉皇殿 (图片提供: FOTOE)
Yudi Hall of Mount Longhu Tao Master Residence (*Tianshi Fu*)

重建,现在的天师府占地4.2万余平方米,尚存古建筑6000余平方米,有500多间房舍。天师府坐北朝南,按照八卦形制,修建了玄坛殿、真武殿、提举署、法箓局、赞教厅、万法宗坛、大堂、家庙、味腴书屋、敕书阁、观星台、纳凉居、灵芝园,以及厢房廊屋等建筑,从而把宫观与王府建筑合为一体。楼台殿阁雄伟壮观,曲径回廊精巧华丽,素有"南国第一家"之称,而府内更是藏有金匾、铜镜、铜钟及天师玉印、三五斩邪雌雄剑等文物珍品。

in ancient times are long gone. Extant structures include some buildings in the magnificent *Shangqing* Temple and Tao Master Residence (*Sihan Tianshi Fu*) which used to be living quarters for Tao masters of different dynasties.

Tao Master Residence (*Tianshi Fu*)

Located at the foot of Mount Longhu, the Tao Master Residence (*Tianshi Fu*), originally known as "Immortal Temple (*Zhenxian Guan*)", was the place where Taoist masters lived and conducted rituals. The magnificent complex faces the Pipa Peak to the south, Mount Xihua to the north and Luxi River in the front. After years of reconstructions, the existing complex occupies an area of 42,000 square meters including 6,000 square meters of ancient structures with 500 rooms. With its back to the north and front to the south, the complex encompasses all buildings in a Taoist eight diagrams layout including Hall of Mysticism (*Xuantan Dian*), Hall of the Great Emperor of Zhenwu (*Zhenwu Dian*), Department of Promotions (*Tiju*

大上清宫

　　大上清宫是著名的道教名观，坐北朝南，占地面积40万平方米，宫殿背靠西华山，南朝琵琶峰，三面环山，一面临水。大上清宫是祖庭天师张道陵及历代天师祈祷和拜神的宗教场所。历代正一道（道教的一支流派）的道人也在这里隐

• 龙虎山大上清宫 (图片提供：FOTOE)
Grand Shangqing Temple (Dashangqing Gong) in Mount Longhu

Shu), Legal Seal Bureau (Fazhuan Ju), Teaching Assistance Bureau (Zanjiao Ting), Dharma Preaching Hall (Wanfa Zongtan), the main hall, the ancestor temple, Weiyu Library (Weiyu Shuwu), Imperial Decrees Library (Chishu Ge), Astronomical Observation Terrace (Guanxing Tai), Cool Air Room (Naliang Ju), and Ganoderma Garden(Lingzhi Yuan) as well as some subsidiary rooms and covered walkways. The Tao Master Residence is known as "the First Household in the South" for its harmonious integration of Taoist temples with imperial architecture style. It has magnificent buildings with exquisitely twisting walkways. It also houses many cultural relics such as gold horizontal tablets, bronze mirrors, bronze bells, jade seals of Taoist masters, and male and female swords against evil spirits.

Grand Shangqing Temple (Dashangqing Gong)

The Grand Shangqing Temple (Dashangqing Gong, literally Grant Heaven Temple) is a well known Taoist temple in an area of 400 square kilometers with its back against Mount Xihua to the north and its front facing the

居练道，修身养性，静心炼丹，是道教文化积淀十分深厚的地方。大上清宫始建于东汉，原为张道陵的草堂，后称"天师草堂"。大上清宫建筑布局呈"八卦"形，是道教独特的古建筑风格。后经过历朝修建，在清朝最鼎盛时期建制设有两宫、十二殿、二十四院，其建制规模不仅在江南称为第一大观，在中国也是首屈一指，故素有"神仙都所"和"百神受职之所"的称誉。

正一观

正一观坐落在龙虎山脚下，始名"天师祖庙"，是第四代天师张盛自四川回龙虎山"永宣祖教"，为祭祀祖天师而建的庙宇。同时，天师张盛还在这里修复祖天师玄坛及丹灶旧址，并在此居住下来，每年三元节时，各地学道者千余人拥向这里。从此，这里宫观林立，道士云集。正一观是龙虎山规模较大、历史悠久的观宇，曾经多次修缮重建，正殿祖师殿供奉张道陵、王长和赵升三人，左右两庑各三间，正门三间，正殿后为玉皇殿，东西坐落着钟鼓楼。

Pipa Peak to the south. It was surrounded by mountains on three sides and river on one side. This was the place where the Taoist ancestor Master Zhang Daoling and other masters paid homage to Taoist deities with their prayers. Believers of *Zhengyi* sect of Taoism school in Chinese Taoism, also enjoyed a secluded life here to practice self-cultivation and make elixir of immortality. First built in the Eastern Han Dynasty, the temple had always been deep rooted in the Taoist culture. It was originally a cottage for Zhang Daoling, known as "the cottage of the celestial master". The temple has a typical ancient Taoist architecture with an eight-diagram layout. After reconstructions in several dynasties, the temple reached its prosperity during the Qing Dynasty (1616-1911) having completed two palaces, twelve halls and twenty-four courtyards. It was the largest Taoist temple site in regions south of the Yangzte River and one of the largest in China known as "the residential capital of deities" and "the place where deities accept duties assigned".

Zhengyi Temple

The *Zhengyi* Temple locates at the foot

of Mount Longhu, originally named the "Ancestor Temple of Celestial Masters" (*Tianshi Zumiao*), it was built by Zhang Sheng, the fourth generation of Taoist masters when he returned from Sichuan Province to preach the ancestor's religion and pay homage to the past Taoist masters. During the same period he restored the original ancient temple of the past masters and settled here. Every year on the 15th day of the first, the seventh and the tenth months of the lunar calendar, thousands of Taoist pilgrims from all over the county came here to visit. Since then many temples sprouted up and a large number of monks gathered here. The *Zhengyi* Temple, rebuilt multiple times, is one of the largest temples in Mount Longhu with a long history. The main hall enshrines Zhang Daoling, Wang Zhang and Zhao Shen. The main hall has covered walkways with three rooms on each side and three rooms in the front. At the rear of the main hall is the Yudi Hall with two bell towers, one in the east and one in the west.

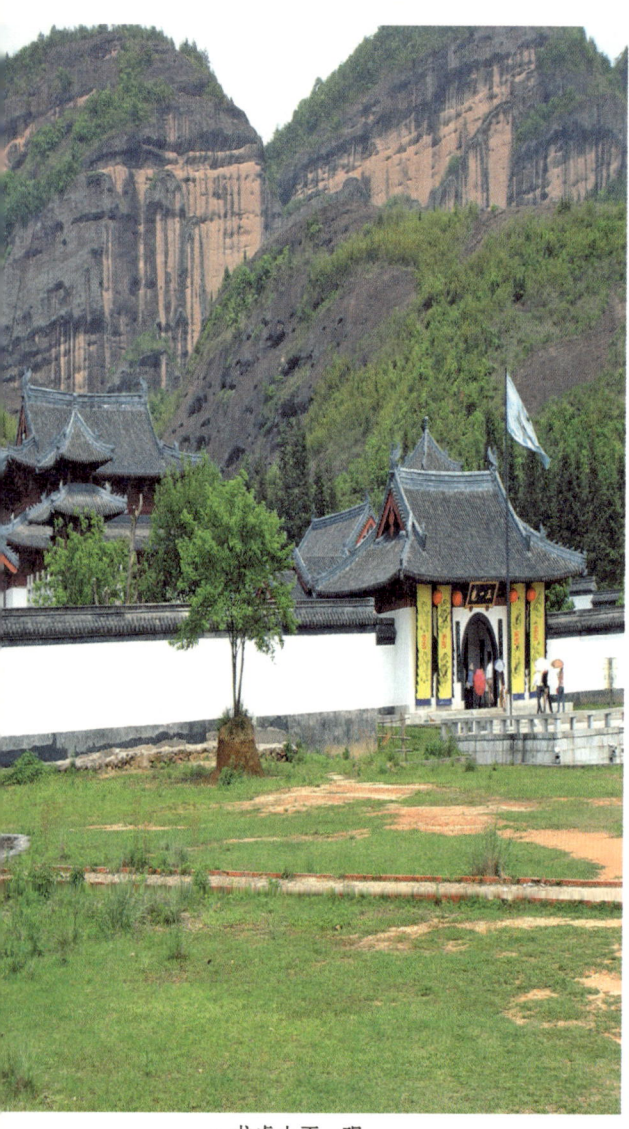

• 龙虎山正一观 (图片提供: FOTOE)
Mount Longhu *Zhengyi* Temple